Looking at Law:
Canada's Legal System

Fifth Edition

Patrick Fitzgerald
Professor of Law, Carleton University
M.A. (Oxon), Barrister-at-Law, Lincoln's Inn,
Member of the Ontario Bar

Barry Wright
Professor of Law, Carleton University
B.A. (Toronto), LL.B. (York), LL.M. (London), D.Jur. (York)

Butterworths

Toronto and Vancouver

Looking at Law: Canada's Legal System, Fifth Edition
© Butterworths Canada Ltd. 2000
August 2000

The Butterworth Group of Companies

Canada:
75 Clegg Road, MARKHAM, Ontario L6G 1A1
and
1721-808 Nelson St., Box 12148, VANCOUVER, B.C. V6Z 2H2
Australia:
Butterworths Pty Ltd., SYDNEY
Ireland:
Butterworth (Ireland) Ltd., DUBLIN
Malaysia:
Malayan Law Journal Sdn Bhd, KUALA LUMPUR
New Zealand:
Butterworths of New Zealand Ltd., WELLINGTON
Singapore:
Butterworths Asia, SINGAPORE
South Africa:
Butterworth Publishers (Pty.) Ltd., DURBAN
United Kingdom:
Butterworth & Co. (Publishers) Ltd., LONDON
United States:
LEXIS Publishing, CHARLOTTESVILLE, Virginia

Canadian Cataloguing in Publication Data

Fitzgerald, Patrick, 1928-
    Looking at law: Canada's legal system

5th ed.
Includes index.
ISBN 0-433-42411-7

1. Law – Canada. I. Wright, Barry, 1957– . II. Title.

KE444.F58 2000   349.71   C00-931745-7
KF385.F58 2000

Printed and bound in Canada.

Dedication

This book is dedicated to the memory of the late King McShane, C.D., B.A., B.C.L., M.A., Adjunct Professor Carleton University and of the Bar of New Brunswick, a valued colleague and friend, who co-authored previous editions of this book.

Preface

This book was first written in 1979 for the Introduction to Legal Studies course at Carleton University. It is intended primarily for first-year university undergraduates. We believe that the book is also useful to students studying law in community colleges or advanced high school settings, and indeed to anyone wishing to know more about Canadian law. Accompanied by more specialized readings, the book also serves as a helpful background text for more advanced studies in law in colleges, universities and professional law schools. The objective of the book is to provide an accessible introductory look at Canada's law, to survey the nature, origins and operation of our legal system, and to address its role in a changing society.

This book is revised extensively from the four previous editions published in 1979, 1982, 1985 and 1994. The authors of the earlier editions, Patrick Fitzgerald and King McShane, accumulated a long list of persons who provided valuable assistance. Professors Graham Parker, David Elliot and Paul Davidson offered helpful suggestions and advice on a number of chapters. Steffi Ortiz, Murray Stephens, Ron Doering, Rosemary Hache, Michael Fitzgerald and Marlene Bradley provided technical assistance on previous editions and Brigid Fitzgerald has continued to do so with this edition. Tim Catherwood, Celia Laframboise, Steven Chisholm and Guy Phillips provided research assistance on previous editions and we would like to give particular thanks to Tim Riordan, now a doctoral student at Simon Fraser University, for research assistance, including updates and inclusions on the topics of alternative dispute resolution, the courts, family law and human rights. Logan Atkinson has provided valuable advice and detailed comments on all chapters in this edition.

Barry Wright would like to express particular thanks to Patrick Fitzgerald and King McShane for the invitation to co-author this major revision of the text. Readers will note that the book is dedicated to the memory of King McShane. His role in the conception and production of the book was considerable and invaluable. We hope that this new edition is faithful to his vision of the book and to his enthusiastic commitment to furthering student legal education.

Patrick Fitzgerald
Barry Wright
Carleton University, 2000

Table of Contents

Chapter Four
The Different Areas of Law: Substantive Law Doctrines

Chapter Five
The Law at Work: Evidence and Procedure

Chapter One

What is Law?

One of the most important and distinctive characteristics of a society is its law. One way in which the human world may be distinguished from the animal world is by the existence of social rules to govern behaviour. In politically organized societies, many of these rules are formalized by the state as laws. These are supplemented by yet further laws as new social interests develop.

The laws and legal systems of various states may be similar, but no two countries have laws that are completely identical. Law, and the authority to make new laws, derives from the particular historical experiences and the constitutional arrangement of a particular country. While Canada's constitution is derived from that of the United Kingdom, Canadian law-making authority is independent and departs from the British model, notably in its federal structure of government and division of law-making responsibilities. The relatively recent introduction of the *Canadian Charter of Rights and Freedoms*,[1] which has made Canadians ever more aware of the law, is yet a further diversion from the British model. Although the United States is also a federal state with a constitutionally entrenched process of judicial review of rights, its constitutional arrangements are very different from Canada's.

There may be basic differences in law within a particular country, too. In Canada, certain laws vary from province to province; Quebec laws on motor accident insurance are quite different from those of Ontario. Laws also vary from community to community; Toronto residents are legally obliged to snow-shovel their sidewalks, Ottawa residents are not.

This book focuses on the common law tradition in Canada. Although common law is the dominant tradition in most of Canada, it is by no means the only tradition. Canada's current laws and institutional arrangements flow from a history of European domination, and we begin to explore the relations between European and pre-existing indigenous laws in Chapter

---

[1] Part I of the *Constitution Act, 1982*, being Schedule B to the *Canada Act 1982* (U.K.), 1982, c. 11.

Two. Canada is a multicultural country; there are different perspectives on the nature of law outside our dominant culture, particularly in non-western traditions.

To a large extent, the law is what defines any society, whether at the community, local, regional or national level. Before we can begin to address the complexity of law in Canada we must confront wider philosophical and theoretical speculations about the law. What, exactly, is law? Is it simply a vast body of rules found in law libraries? Can law be understood simply as an authoritative process of dispute-resolution? What is its relationship to abstract ideals such as justice and morality? How is it connected to the realities of political power and social practices? What does law achieve and how can it be improved?

Not surprisingly, there are an enormous range of answers to these questions. However, at the risk of great simplification and generalization, explanations of the law and its purposes may be broken down into two approaches, jurisprudential and interdisciplinary.

Traditionally, the branch of legal scholarship concerned with wider speculative questions about the law is known as jurisprudence. Jurisprudential approaches to law tend to be "internal", meaning that they look to law itself for explanations. They seek to deal with the question, what is law? by separating it from other practices and institutions. Since the late nineteenth century, particularly in the last 30 years, scholars working in disciplines outside of law have also attempted to address questions about the nature and purpose of law. These interdisciplinary approaches to law tend to be "external", drawing explanations from analyses of the role of the legal system in its social, political, economic and cultural context.

I. JURISPRUDENTIAL CONCEPTIONS OF LAW

A. Law, Morality and Natural Law

Some legal scholars argue that, despite the technical complexity of law, it is in essence concerned with right and wrong. Is law not related to our duties to our neighbours, a sort of applied morality?

Many would argue that there is a connection between law and morality. Some ancient and medieval philosophers such as Cicero, Augustine and Aquinas went so far as to claim that law and morality are essentially identical. In their opinion "positive" law (the law laid down in any particular country) must conform to "natural" law (universal moral principles discoverable by the correct exercise of the intellect). If positive law fails to conform to natural law principles, it fails to be true or legitimate law. On this basis Nazis condemned for their treatment of the Jewish people could not defend themselves by saying they were obeying Hitler's laws, since these were too immoral to qualify as laws in failing to respect human dignity, rights and the sanctity of life. According to the natural law tradition, an unjust law is not a law at all.

Clearly, morality and law are interrelated. However, they are not identical. First, morality is only concerned with right and wrong, good and evil; law is concerned with many things that do not involve right and wrong. For instance, procedures for land registration and incorporation have no obvious relationship to morality.

Second, morality is often vague, understood only in very general terms, rather than in great detail. Law, on the other hand, is required to be specific. For example, when are children old enough to be held responsible for their misdeeds? Morally, it all depends upon the child's rate of development; legally, certainty and consistency require that an arbitrary line be drawn at a specific age (in common law, seven) below which a child can incur no criminal liability.

Third, much of modern thought about morality concludes that morality is relative, dependent on the subjective views of individuals. Since the nineteenth century, it has become increasingly hard to identify a shared moral code. For this reason, morality is often considered uncertain. Law, however, is supposed to be clearly discernible and objective. Does the sanctity of life extend to the unborn and how is it to be measured against the rights of the mother? How are the interests protected by censorship, obscenity and sedition laws to be weighed against concerns about freedom of expression? While many traditionalists and social conservatives have clear positions on these issues, some even arguing that their positions should be law, most recognize that these are contentious matters, involving competing considerations, and that differences in opinion should not be punished by the law.

There are many areas of morality where differences of opinion and action need to be respected if a society is to be considered free. Law relates to disputes that can be authoritatively decided by judges, whereas moral controversies can go on forever, as they no doubt will on matters such as abortion, sexuality and other personal lifestyle choices. The distinction is important because the consequences of breaking a moral rule may be quite different than the consequences of breaking a law. The former may result in a struggle of conscience or perhaps community disapproval, while the latter will invite the intervention of the state and the imposition of punishment in the form of fines or imprisonment. For this reason, Pierre Trudeau famously observed that the state has no business in the bedrooms of the nation.

When the law does attempt to impose what are perceived to be the dominant moral standards of a particular time, it often fails to adjust as those dominant moral standards change. The law usually fails to keep pace with change and is often difficult to reform. As a result, the rigidity of law embodying earlier dominant moral codes results in injustice. For example, the common law spousal immunity rule in rape cases was at one time considered to be consistent with morality by those who dominated the state. A man could not be convicted of forcible non-consented intercourse with his wife. The view that, by marriage, women implied consent to all sexual advances from their husbands, and the implication that they were mere property of their spouse, were challenged in the late nineteenth century. However, it took Canada's criminal law until 1984 to change the legal rule. Similarly, Canada's *Indian Act* at one time specified that aboriginal women marrying non-natives lost their Indian status while aboriginal men retained their status in the same situation. The Supreme Court of Canada declared the law discriminatory in 1974, but the legislation was not changed by Parliament until 1985.

Modern natural law advocates, such as Patrick Devlin and J.M. Finnis, argue that there remain ultimate moral principles that the law must reflect and according to which social behaviour must be judged, although religion no longer forms the basis of these moral principles in our secular society. These principles bind society together, and without supporting them by the force of law, society would soon disintegrate. What these ultimate principles are and how far they are to extend in the law is unclear. However, it is also unclear how law and morality can be completely segregated on matters such as violent offences, human rights, family obligations, commercial honesty and so on.

B. Law as Sovereign Commands

The jurisprudential tradition associated with legal positivism attempts to draw a clear distinction between law and morality. It does this by focusing on what "is" (laws as they are actually enacted by an accepted authority) rather than on what "ought to be" (laws that should derive from human nature and morality). According to the legal positivists, law is not a set of propositions derived and evaluated from common moral standards but an organized set of rules enacted and enforced by a recognized authority. They are valid simply because they are enacted by accepted authority, enforced by this authority, and generally obeyed. This positivist approach avoids many of the problems identified in the last section while introducing new ones.

The founder of legal positivism was Jeremy Bentham, a British utilitarian philosopher and reformer in late eighteenth and early nineteenth centuries. Influenced by the Enlightenment, he energetically rejected the natural law tradition and William Blackstone's celebration of obscure common law. Law should not be evaluated by a judge or scholar's view of what "ought" to be, but rather by a certain and systematic analysis of what actually exists. The law should be judged by how well it accords to the principles of utility, defined primarily in terms of maximizing happiness for the greatest number.

John Austin expanded these ideas, describing law as a system of official rules generated by the state. Whether a provision such as that in the *Indian Act* is just depends upon its content, but whether it is law depends upon its pedigree: was it enacted by an authoritative legislature according to the proper procedures? According to Austin, "the existence of a law is one thing, its merit or demerit is quite another." The latter questions may be debated in the political sphere of parliament, but not in the courts. Positive laws are those rules which issued from established constitutional or sovereign authority and no other rules or laws are enforceable by the courts.

It is a short step from the views of Bentham and Austin to the modern concept of the rule of law, as articulated by A.V. Dicey in the late nineteenth century. Government according to the rule of law means that power is exercised according to laws generated by duly constituted authority (whether through the constitution, legislation or judicial precedent) and not the arbitrary discretion of powerful persons. All government actions must be justified by legal authority and take place within the framework of legal rules. No person is above positive law and all such laws are to be administered by an independent judiciary.

Legal positivism, or law as sovereign commands, presents the law as an autonomous system of official rules that may be judged according to purely constitutional and technical requirements, while avoiding value judgements of morality, justice and equity. However, in practice, law is often bound up with these latter concerns. Law is not just a set of rules that may or may not conform with concepts of justice. On the contrary, one of its objectives is the achievement of justice. This is reflected in our language when we refer to ministries of justice, courts of justice, criminal justice. It is reflected in the oaths sworn by judges aiming to achieve justice in their courts. It is reflected in popular criticism when justice is perceived to be denied.

While a technically valid law can be unjust, a legal system completely oriented to injustice is unimaginable, although the example of the Nazis shows that some systems have come close. Their actions may have been supported by laws validly enacted within their system, but such laws certainly offend our sense of justice and indeed the value placed on human rights increasingly recognized in international law.

When faced with a legal problem, the student will tend to fly to encyclopaedias, statutes and cases for the answer. This is the tradition of legal positivism at work, the notion that there is nothing more to law than what can be read in the record of laws given the blessing of an accepted authority. But more experienced hands know better. They start by reflecting on the facts of the problem, weighing both sides of the question, considering the demands of fairness and justice in the situation and arrive at a conclusion based on principle. Then, they turn to the law books to see whether the conclusion is supported by statutes and cases. This latter approach recognizes that perhaps there is more to law than the way it appears from a review of laws approved by the accepted authority. Sometimes the law needs to be corrected or adjusted and this does not always take place exclusively through the passage of sovereign acts of legislation. Many of the most influential appeal cases, court decisions that have fundamentally changed the way we understand the law, have involved principles derived from justice, fairness and common sense rather than technical questions resolvable by looking at the law as it "is". Familiar rules such as "finders keepers", "no-one can give who doesn't already have", "no-one shall profit from their own crime" derive from such broad principles and are not articulated clearly in the law, despite their influence on many important legal decisions.

C. Law as Rules

H.L.A. Hart has developed a more sophisticated positivist concept of law. This concept sets out a hierarchy of rules and accommodates the fact that people not only obey or act according to rules, as Austin assumed, but also have a "reflective attitude" towards them. Hart separates law and morality for the purpose of analysis but also attempts to accommodate the more awkward questions about justice raised above. Law consists not only of rules but also principles. According to Hart, principles are themselves rules of a general kind that underlie the more specific rules which constitute most of our law.

Rules are, of course, familiar features of the social landscape. We have rules of grammar, spelling, etiquette, games, clubs, morality and law. Indeed, social life without rules is hardly conceivable. Law can be said to be comprised basically of rules but Hart's concept of law pushes analysis of rules and their social function yet further. For Hart, rules are social phenomena that have an internal and external aspect.

First, the external aspect. To say that there is such and such a rule in any given society is to say something about people's actual behaviour in that society. It is to say that in general its members act in such and such a way. In other words it is to say that, in a certain respect, their behaviour converges. Put another way, the external aspect of rules relates to the way rules affect people's behaviour without reference to their own individual consideration of how they ought to behave. In this respect, rules are external to individual deliberations about behaviour.

The internal aspect of rules, on the other hand, reflects something about how people think they ought to behave. Saying that there is a rule governing a certain type of behaviour also says something about accepted views about behaviour. It relates not only to actual behaviour but to the behaviour thought to be required of a society. It tells us that deviations from the required standard are liable to be met with criticism and disapproval.

Let us take an example: the rules of the road. In Canada driving on the right is required by law. In the United Kingdom driving on the left is not absolutely required by law but is a rule of custom. This means two things. First, it is to say that in general British motorists do drive on the left; if they drove on the right, as in Canada, the rule would be different. Second, it is to say that motorists drive on the left, not just out of habit, but out of a conviction that they ought to do so because this is required of them. Rules, then, whether of grammar, morality or law, have two sides to them. One side relates to practice and actual behaviour. The other is a sense of obligation concerning what should or must be done.

However, law is more than just a set of unrelated separate rules. The rules that constitute a country's law are organized and knit together into a coherent structure. For this reason a country's law is frequently referred to as its legal system. But what is it that gives order, structure and coherence to a set of legal rules? What is it that welds them into a legal system? Two features, it is suggested: first, its higher-order rules, and second, its basic principles.

Higher-order rules have been touched on already to some extent in the discussion of the difference between law and morality. The morality of a society may consist of customary rules. If, however, it consisted only of such rules, law would come into controversy as it tends to change and develop very gradually. New laws could not be created when necessary, old laws could not be abolished, and there would be no possibility of speedy amendment. As it is, however, law admits of alteration by a variety of methods through legislation or court decisions. In other words, law contains higher-order rules which provide methods for making, unmaking and changing all the other rules.

Legal rules are also welded together by basic principles. These are very general rules relating to fairness and justice that provide the underpinning for the more specific legal rules. They help to unify law in two ways. First, they give reason, purpose and direction to rules, particularly judge-made rules. Second, they underlie, at one and the same time, rules in many different areas of law.

D. Law as Rights and Modern Concepts of Justice

For some legal scholars, Hart's analytically complex concept of rules fails to adequately respond to the shortcomings of legal positivism. Justice based on positive law alone remains unsatisfactory and the search continues for underlying value-based principles that can be given objective positive content. R.M. Dworkin's search focuses on controversial cases involving uncertain law. Such cases challenge the positivist separation of "is" and "ought".

Dworkin accepts that, while valid rules of law may guide most cases, "hard" cases, about which most informed people may reasonably disagree, involve reference to standards that are not rules. Such standards may be policies, principles of justice or fairness, or some other dimension of morality. A judge faced with a difficult case will not simply refer to applicable rules. The case may be difficult precisely because there may be no applicable rules or because the rules are subject to some relevant exception. The judge will turn to the underlying purpose or policy of the rules in the area or to some other standard to achieve a just and fair result.

Once we accept that law consists of other standards as well as rules, "ought" questions return. The challenge that remains is how these standards that help resolve hard cases are to be determined objectively. Dworkin does not suggest community opinion polls or reference to some common moral code, as advocated by natural law scholars. Rather he suggests that the appropriate approach involves a judicial consideration of rights. What standard would fit consistently with the abstract rights to which a community has already committed itself in its constitution and institutional practices?

Problems remain with Dworkin's focus on judges and the judge's consideration and balancing of rights. While judges have legal expertise and experience with the complexities of achieving justice, they are also human beings with subjective views on the recognition and weighing of rights. How do judges distinguish between fundamental rights and rights that are legal and political constructs? Moreover, the judge-centred focus of Dworkin's analysis is confined to adversarial approaches to justice, where one party wins and the other loses. Many hard cases do not go to the courts at all. (Restorative justice, or the results achieved by mediation or arbitration processes, may involve a very different weighing of rights than that exercised by a judge.)

II. INTERDISCIPLINARY APPROACHES TO LAW

Although jurisprudential approaches to law offer an array of answers to the question "what is law?" the perspectives surveyed may be seen to fall into two camps: (1) variations on the theme that law ultimately involve reference to a core of principles where "ought" questions are considered, and (2) variations on the theme that law is made up of rules that are best discerned and explained by a focus on the law as enacted by an accepted authority reference to what "is". Both approaches focus on internal or doctrinally oriented questions about law. Legal rules and principles are the objects of reasoning, the focus of speculation, and the source of truth. Jurisprudence tends to focus on issues such as legal status, powers and obligations. By contrast, interdisciplinary approaches to law tend to focus on issues such as function, interest, group and class. The interdisciplinary approaches also emphasize examination of the actual practices in the legal system and the roles performed by law in society, matters which are of secondary importance in jurispudence.

Some philosophers deal with the general difficulty of definition in philosophy by asserting, "If you want to know what philosophy is, go and find out what philosophers do." Likewise, another approach to finding out what law is about is to examine what lawyers and judges do. As we will see in Chapter Seven, "law jobs" are many and varied. The most important is negotiating and settling disputes. In court, judges make authoritative resolutions and lawyers engage in advocacy — appearing as prosecuting law officers of the crown and defending accused in criminal cases, representing plaintiffs and defendants in civil cases. Most cases, though, never reach the courts. Much of a lawyer's work is done outside the courts and in the office advising clients, telling them their rights and obligations, explaining the law, negotiating for them in their disputes with others and predicting the prospects of litigation. Not that lawyers are exclusively concerned with disputes. Much of their work has to do with non-contentious matters, transactions such as land sales and purchases, registration of mortgages, drafting of wills and flotation of companies. Many lawyers working in private firms, for the government or for corporations, rarely, if ever, go to court.

Jurisprudential definitions of law tend to involve assumptions about the role of law in society. These assumptions are not necessarily wrong, but are based on concepts drawn from how the law itself describes society. Most legal scholars assume, and some scholars from other disciplines agree, that the law's performance of social, political and economic functions reflect agreement or broad consensus in society. Resolving individual disputes in a controlled way helps to integrate society. However, other scholars argue that the law serves dominant interests, authoritatively performing these roles in order to reinforce inequalities in society.

Social life involves conflicting purposes, competition for scarce resources, and disagreements over how things should be done. Such conflict defines us as humans. Social scientists problematize these conflicts and the way law deals with them. Does the law resolve minor, largely individual conflicts in ways that minimize social disruption and in a fashion that legitimately accords with common values of respect, justice and fairness? Or does the law deal with conflicts that reflect deeper divisions in society and in a manner that promotes powerful interests? These questions about the role of law extend beyond the nature of society. What is the role of law in organizing state institutions and authorizing the exercise of state power? What is the role of law in carrying out the complex transactions needed in a modern industrial society?

Interdisciplinary approaches step outside an internalized focus on law and attempt to explicitly address such questions. They define the law by examining what actually takes place in the legal system and attempting to analyze its functions or roles in social, political, economic and cultural life. The interdisciplinary approaches emphasize the legal system rather than law because inquiry is not confined to legal doctrines but includes an examination of legal institutions and personnel. Social and political theorists, historians and economists are all interested in knowing what law is and the role and nature of the legal system in relation to the matters within their own disciplines. These interests are shared by legal scholars who are sceptical of the claims and assumptions of traditional or mainstream professional legal scholarship, and who have wider interests in the contexts of the legal system.

A. Legal Realism, Sociological Jurisprudence and Critical Legal Studies

The legal realist movement is primarily associated with a pragmatic, sceptical school of legal scholarship that emerged in the United States in the early twentieth century. The American legal realists emphasized the failure of legal doctrine to predict practical legal outcomes; predictable results do not follow from the application of legal doctrine to factual problems. Legal results can be best understood through an empirical understanding of external circumstances such as the values held by judges and political and economic pressures. There is little objectivity in determining facts and doctrine mostly serves to justify or legitimate the result. The realists emphasized law as a product of experience, rather than logic (Oliver Wendell Holmes), sought to understand "law in action" as opposed to law as it was "found in the books" (Karl Llewellyn), and extended their skepticism of legal rules to the manner in which facts are determined in the legal process (Jerome Frank).

In some respects, particularly in the association of legal realists and progressive law reform, the American legal realists were similar to the utilitarian Jeremy Bentham, who sought to clear away the vague accumulated "nonsense" of common law over a century earlier, and focus on humans' rational behaviour. They are also linked with the work of their contemporary, Roscoe Pound, who is most often associated with the phrase "sociological jurisprudence". The legal scholar should not reconstruct the meaning of law from legal texts but rather survey and classify the social interests served by law, study the actual historical effects of doctrine and legal institutions, and examine ways to make the law more effective through an active agenda of reform.

The critical legal studies (CLS) movement is the most recent manifestation of the sceptical tradition in American legal scholarship. It updates the realists by drawing upon modern social and cultural theory and attempting to deconstruct the seemingly objective language of the law. They demonstrate how particular social interests are covertly promoted while others are nullified through unchallenged doctrinal conceptualizations and legal processes.

Unlike the realists and Pound, the CLS scholars are pessimistic about the progressive possibilities of law reform without wider political, economic and social change. What all these scholars share is a sceptical or critical approach to internal law. Their analysis of law's relation to its broader context is varied. Conceptions of the legal system developed by social theorists are more developed and coherent in this respect.

B. Social Theory and Law

For many social scientists, the question "what is law?" is an important way of confronting other questions about how society is organized. E.A. Hoebel, the mid-twentieth century anthropologist, suggested that social norms are legal if their neglect or violation are met with punishment by individuals or groups with socially-recognized authority. Such a definition places law at the centre of how a society is organized (questions of authority and social order) and suggests something about the social function of law.

One of the first scholars to pursue these issues in a coherent and systematic way was the late nineteenth century French sociologist Emile Durkheim. His central concern related to the question, "what holds a society together?" Durkheim drew a distinction between "primitive" and "advanced" societies. In the former, the majority work toward common aims and acknowledge that a society's moral and legal code are necessary to keep it together. Where there is departure from these expressions of solidarity, criminal sanctions are imposed. These repressive laws not only punish the offender but reinforce the boundaries between acceptable and unacceptable behaviour and help to maintain the cohesion of the whole social group. In advanced societies, where there is a complex economy of specialized production and divided labour, there is also a change in the nature of social solidarity. In advanced societies, law accordingly becomes more complex. Repressive laws are increasingly displaced by ones that compensate rather than punish, in other words, laws that restore the complainant to the position he or she was before the dispute. From these functions the basic divide between criminal and civil law emerges. Durkheim thought that criminal laws would wither away as societies became more complex, a prediction that has not held true.

Karl Marx, a German theorist active at roughly the same time as Durkheim, did not develop a social theory of law, despite studying law early in his life. However, he did develop an analysis of society that was very influential. Many of his followers extended his analysis to the role of law. Marx articulated a "conflict" analysis of society based on what was claimed to be a scientific study of the history of social relations and the material conditions of humanity. Durkheim tended to assume that "consensus" and shared values are the norm in society, and that social conflicts are mostly superficial disputes that the law resolves before they become socially disruptive. For Marx, conflicts reveal the real nature of society, rooted in the fundamental realities of production in the economy. In the capitalist economy of Marx's time, the emergence of urban industrial factories pooled resources and labour power on an unprecedented scale. The owners of the means of production extracted enormous profits by exploiting workers who added their labour value to production. The law and the other institutions of the state were seen as part of the super-structure that maintained this inequitable situation based on social relations and the means of production.

Marx rashly predicted that an imminent crisis in capitalism would lead to revolution and the withering away of law. As a result, he said little specifically about the law although numerous Marxist conceptions of law have since developed. Some argue that it is best understood by looking to the practices of law in self-described communist states. Other Marxist theorists such as E.B. Pashukanis emphasize that basic function of law is to reduce all social relations and their products to mere commodity forms and values. Other Marxists such as A. Gramsci argue that law, in addition to preserving the status quo of inequality through repression and other instrumental means, also disguises the nature of inequality by ideologically shaping how people comprehend the world around them.

Max Weber, a German scholar, is perhaps the most influential theorist of the sociology of law. While Durkheim had a consensus view and Marx a conflict view, Weber could be described as adhering to a "pluralist" view of society. Weber accepted that there are fundamental conflicting social interests that go well beyond individual disputes. However, the law and other institutions are remarkably successful in brokering these conflicts, producing enough equilibrium to preclude the threat of revolutionary change. Unlike Marx, Weber rejected the economy as the sole or primary influence on law but saw a constellation of influences including the economy, technology, politics and ideology.

In order to examine complex social phenomena, Weber postulated ideal types or abstract analytical categories. Applying these to questions of power, he described three forms of authority. Under traditional domination, legal and political authority is legitimated by the sanctity of tradition and historical practice. Under charismatic domination, legal and political authority is legitimated by the exceptional personality of individual leaders. Under legal domination, authority is legitimated by the law itself.

The law has developed a high degree of formality and rationality and is obeyed precisely because it is perceived to be impersonal and rational. "Formal legal rationality" relates to third "ideal type" of analysis, characterized by formal processes by which decisions are arived at rationally by specialist personnel. A number of features of formal legal rationality follow from this. While repressive laws continue to exist, and all laws serve particular groups more than others, "facilitative" laws, such as those relating to contract, generate the appearance that all individual interests are served. Another feature of formal legal rationality is the emphasis on formal legal equality, the concept that all persons have the same rights, which obscures the reality of social inequalities. Yet another characteristic is the prominence of legal professionals who administer the law in bureaucracies that operate autonomously from the political sphere. For Weber, then, law is central to authority in modern society.

While the social theorists Durkheim, Marx and Weber and their followers have generated an enormous quantity of literature about the law, there have been numerous modern challenges to these social theories. Most notable are feminist and post-modern approaches which cannot be easily absorbed within the older theoretical traditions. Feminist theorists reveal significant omissions and the post-modernists question the very possibility of a "scientific" study of society.

It is obvious that Durkheim, Marx and Weber said very little about gender and the role of women within their conceptions of law and society. A number of scholars have developed explanatory theories that go beyond describing examples of discrimination in the administration of law and in the attitudes of lawyers and judges as merely manifestations of sexism. Carol Smart and Catherine Mackinnon are feminist theorists who explain how laws and legal language construct and perpetuate patriarchal social relations. While conceding that modern legal reforms increasingly recognize equal rights and have reduced the cruder forms of discrimination, they point out that such measures usually fail to confront the social realities of unequal power. We also see the growth of legal regulation around the lives of women, affecting matters such as reproductive and sexual freedoms.

The recent emergence of post-modern theories have also had an impact on theories of law, notably through the work of Michel Foucault. Postmodernism takes a sceptical stance towards the possibilities of comprehensive rational explanations of social phenomena, rejecting, as some put it, the ambitious "Enlightenment projects" of social science. Foucault emphasizes the complexity of modern social and institutional development. Not all changes in social ordering are orchestrated by a monolithic state acting as a controlling agent of particular social groups. Nor are they implemented through formal law. They are generated by a range of social practices, notably in discursive and cultural forms, that lie beyond and stand in uncertain relation to more formal manifestations of power. While Weber saw an expansion of the role of law in modernity, Foucault suggests it plays a declining role, as cruder mechanisms of governance of others are displaced by the more subtle mechanisms of governance of the self.

C. Other Perspectives

There are other disciplines, in addition to those associated with social theory, that have developed interest in the definition and roles of law. Historians, political scientists, economists and literary scholars tend not to articulate their definitions of law in the same way as social theorists or scholars of jurisprudence. Their definitions are nonetheless implicit in the questions they ask about the law.

Historians, for instance, have come to recognize the centrality of law to social and political developments (indeed, Marx and Weber considered themselves historians as well as social theorists). Legal history within traditional legal scholarship tended to be pre-occupied with doctrinal developments and the medieval foundations of common law. The impact of realist and critical legal scholarship has seen the growth of new legal history which examines matters such as the relationship of law to modern economic development and the emergence of professions (*e.g.*, W. Hurst, M.J. Horwitz, D. Sugarman). Social historians such as E.P. Thompson, J.M. Beattie and D. Hay concerned about the lives of those who left few records of their own, have discovered that the records of the criminal courts shed light on those lives and on the uses of law in the exercise of authority.

Other scholars share the historians' interest in law. Political scientists are interested in law because of its role in the exercise and management of political power. Federalism and human rights in Canada cannot be understood without reference to constitutional documents and the record of judicial review. Economists are interested in law because of its role in the structuring of economic behaviour. The "law and economics" movement is a highly developed field of scholarship that studies the the relationship of economic considerations such as efficiency and certainty to private and regulatory laws (*e.g.*, R. Posner, P. Atiyah). Literary scholars are interested in how dramas involving justice and morality unfold in the legal system as well as in the legal controls over freedom of expression.

There are numerous ways to approach and understand the law, both within traditional professional legal scholarship and from the perspectives of other disciplines. We see that the basic question, "what is law?", gives rise to numerous philosophical and theoretical responses.

They are constructed out of subsidiary questions that reflect the particular interests of the scholar posing the question. In becoming exposed to these responses many students of law end up with more questions than answers. This is only appropriate. While these speculative questions should remain at the forefront for anyone entering the world of law, this world becomes clearer as we start to examine the details of its operation.

FURTHER READING

R. Cotterrell, *The Sociology of Law: An Introduction* (London: Butter-worths, 1984)

R. Dworkin, *Taking Rights Seriously* (London: Duckworth, 1977)

P. Fitzgerald, *This Law of Ours* (Scarborough: Prentice-Hall of Canada, 1977)

J.W. Harris, *Legal Philosophies* (London: Butterworths, 1980)

P. Harris, *Law in Context: An Introduction to Law* (London: Weidenfeld and Nicolson, 1984)

H.L.A. Hart, *The Concept of Law* (Oxford: Clarendon, 1976)

A. Hunt, *The Sociological Movement in Law* (London: Macmillan, 1978)

D. Lloyd, *The Idea of Law* (London: Penguin, 1973)

S.M. Waddams, *Introduction to the Study of Law* (Toronto: Carswell, 1992)

Chapter Two

How Canada Received Its Law

Law, as suggested in Chapter One, is part of what defines a country. Art historian John Ruskin said, "...nations write their autobiographies in three manuscripts — the book of their deeds, the book of their words and the book of their art." To these three books we could add a fourth: the book of their laws. Canada's book of laws is a curious one. For one thing, it misses some important pages, for another, it is written in two different styles. Thirdly, the narrative details undergo continual revision and occasional transformation.

I. THE IMPOSITION OF EUROPEAN LAW

Anyone opening a nation's book of laws would expect to find a largely home-grown product reflecting contributions from the peoples making up that nation. In Canada, however, our state law is far from being a home-grown product. Indeed it is, like many other of our institutions, almost entirely imported. English common law, and, in the case of Quebec, French civil law, form the primary basis of modern Canadian law. The laws and formal practices of our first nations or aboriginal peoples, while recognized in early treaties, were neglected by British North American and Canadian courts and governments. This neglect is only beginning to be corrected. How much our legal system will accommodate indigenous rights and customs as articulated in nation to nation treaties remains to be seen.

Legal scholars use the term reception to describe the process by which European laws were introduced. Discussion of the issue tends to convey the impression that laws were adopted in a vacuum, that the territories were for all intents and purposes legally vacant. Reception is in fact bound up with the political realities of conquest and the imposition of an outside legal order.

In the seventeenth and eighteenth centuries, powerful European countries, notably Britain, France and Spain, competed over trade and the acquisition of territories in North America. In order to minimize conflict, international law required these imperial powers to conclude treaties with local populations, unless the territory could be considered "juridically vacant", in other words, there was no recognizable political and legal order.

Explorer Samuel du Champlain patronizingly observed: "They [the natives he encountered] are for the most part a people that has no law." His reference point was, of course, French law. Early anthropologists such as E.A. Hoebel and Diamond Jenness recognized the developed sense and craft of law possessed by North American aboriginal nations, with well-developed rules about property, hunting and the environment in particular. The imperial powers had less enlightened insights, but they soon recognized that the conclusion of treaties implicitly recognizing native people as nations with their own laws, in territories they wished to exploit, would give them advantages over their European competitors. In what we now know as Canada, the *Royal Proclamation of 1763* formed the most important base of such agreements. Treaties of friendship and trade had been concluded before this date but the proclamation set up a process of transferring title to the crown in return for protection of aboriginal land use, self-government and the preserving of other native rights in trust.

The *Royal Proclamation of 1763* followed the British conquest of Quebec four years earlier, and was an attempt to better secure Britain's hold over eastern North America. Native alliances were concluded and English laws were to prevail in areas of European trade and settlement to the degree local authorities deemed appropriate. Pre-existing legal systems, both aboriginal and French, were tolerated, although British subjects were entitled to the rights and benefits of English common law and statutes.

Once European settlement in British colonies reached significant levels, there were demands for constitutional protection of legal rights in the form of representative political institutions and courts to regularly administer laws. At this point, a colony went through "formal reception". All English laws and statutes up to the date a colonial legislature and legal system were established became the basis of that colony's law, to be modified and added to by the local legislature and courts as local conditions required (resulting in some important early departures from English law). Quebec quickly went through formal reception under the *Quebec Act, 1774*[1] and, as the French population was large and influential, British authorities recognized that compromise was prudent. French civil law was preserved for

---

[1] (U.K.), 14 Geo. III, c. 83.

matters other than criminal law. The influx of loyalist refugees escaping the American revolution led to the creation of Upper Canada, modern day Ontario, from the western portions of Quebec; and New Brunswick from the western portions of Nova Scotia, which had gone through formal reception in 1758. Like Nova Scotia and unlike Quebec, Upper Canada adopted the full array of English law when it went through formal reception in 1791. Newfoundland followed suit in 1832, British Columbia in 1858 and Manitoba, Saskatchewan, Alberta, the Northwest Territories and Yukon Territories in 1870.

These developments had a negative effect on the first nations of Canada. The British North American colonies resisted recognition of aboriginal rights after they went through formal reception. The British Crown, which had concluded treaties, tended to be negligent in its trusteeship of native rights. By the nineteenth century, political pressures were such that the demands of European settlers in the colonies took precedence (the *Royal Proclamation of 1763* had earlier fuelled one of the grievances leading to the American Revolution), strategic native alliances were no longer important to the British government, and many of the first nations were in decline, devastated by newly-introduced diseases and deepening conflicts between their lifestyle and the emerging economic priorities of European settlers.

With Confederation and the creation of the Dominion of Canada in 1867, the federal government took on the Crown's responsibilities for native affairs and treaty obligations. Native peoples were registered under the *Indian Act* and regulated by paternalistic administrative measures of segregation and assimilation. Ottawa, and indeed most people of European background at the time, saw these measures as civilizing. Native peoples experienced them as devastating and destructive to their culture. They were regulated by a huge array of incomprehensible foreign rules that they had little or no hand in shaping. The courts continued to neglect treaty obligations until relatively recently. The constitution was largely silent on native rights until 1982 when sections 25 and 35 of the *Canadian Charter of Rights and Freedoms*[2] reiterated legal obligations taken on over 200 years earlier but largely ignored in the meantime.

The missing pages of native contributions to the formal state laws of Canada are only beginning to be filled. Traditional native conceptions of the environment, economic activity, ownership and community differ radically from, and may, in some respects, be superior to, the competitive, exploitative

---

[2] Part I of the *Constitution Act, 1982*, being Schedule B to the *Canada Act 1982* (U.K.), 1982, c. 11.

European approaches that have dominated for over two centuries. Some native laws and customs have been remarkably resilient and have been preserved within native communities. However, many native traditions may be difficult if not impossible to recover for the simple reason that they have been suppressed, sometimes violently, and distorted by European contact for so many years. Before native approaches can make a more substantial contribution to formal Canadian law in the future, our courts and legislatures must take further steps to redress wrongs, settle land claims, and empower native communities. The historical failure to let natives contribute their insights to Canadian state laws has done our society a disservice. More serious still is the disservice to the first nations.

II. THE COMMON LAW AND CIVIL LAW TRADITIONS

Aside from missing pages, Canada's book of law is unusual in another way: it is written in two quite different styles. Canada is not only bilingual but also "bijural". We have two different legal systems, one in Quebec and the other in the rest of Canada. As suggested above, Quebec retains a substantial part of the type of law brought by the settlers from France through the *Quebec Act, 1774*. The rest of Canada retains the legal system brought from England and fully adopted at the time of formal reception. The difference between French civil law and English common law may be grasped by surveying hundreds of years of European history.

As the Dark Ages gave way to the medieval period in Europe, universities emerged in various cities. Students seeking to enter official service as judges, counsellors or ministers studied three subjects above all: theology, medicine and law. The law they studied was not local or national laws, which were chaotic, uncertain and fragmented. The law they studied was abstract and idealistic, built on common sense notions of morality and justice, Christian doctrines and Roman law. A vast repository of written laws survived the fall of the Roman Empire and the Middle Ages. The law of the Roman citizens, the *jus civile* (civil law), had been developed over the centuries by Roman jurists, who fashioned it largely in the course of discussing legal problems with their students.

Actual local and national laws continued to be the diet of the courts that adjudicated according to local customs. In 1215, clerics were forbidden to take part in trial by ordeal (the resort to torture in legal proceedings) and there was growing pressure to bring more rationality to law. A new comprehensive system of law could be built out of existing customs, or alternatively, Roman law could be reinstated. The latter approach was championed by the universities, and prevailed. Roman law was adapted to national conditions and systematized into codes. The modern European legal systems have their roots in these codes, which were brought by European settlers to South America, Mexico, Quebec and to other areas of French and Spanish colonization. As well, European legal systems were exported to countries such as Turkey and Japan, which modelled their own laws on codes of continental Europe. So civil law became the dominant legal system with the notable exception of the English-speaking countries (apart from Scotland which, like Quebec, has a civil law system based on Roman law).

England also sent scholars to the medieval European universities. Unlike the other European countries, England was an isolated island subjugated by the most energetic and powerful dynasty of the age, William the Conqueror and his successors. The courts set up to consolidate his dynasty's rule proved to be remarkably effective, doing away with the need for a large standing army of Norman occupation. Local agents, justices of the peace, were appointed to administer the courts in every county and to preside over trials of minor matters as magistrates. Upstanding local citizens were enlisted to assist in these functions as jurors, sheriffs, constables. Royally appointed judges based in London were sent out annually on circuit to all the different counties to oversee regional administration and deal with more serious offences and local disputes. In doing so, the judges gradually built up a law that was not particular to any locality, but common to the whole realm.

English common law, therefore, originated not with teachers but with judges. Faced with disputes between litigants, the judges searched for fair, just and reasonable solutions, which they made up as they went along, relying on their own sense of justice. Since justice requires like cases to be treated alike, the judges sought consistency and uniformity by following previous decisions. A body of law was built up fashioned by powerful and prestigious royal judges. It became so well-established that when Europe abandoned local customs for Roman law, England had a national system strong enough to resist the tide. Civil law had little impact, common law was developed, and in due course was brought by British subjects and by conquest to Ireland, the American colonies, Australia, New Zealand and Canada.

Through the retention of civil law in Quebec, Canada has maintained both influential legal systems. We have the civil law of Roman ancestry, begotten by professors and raised on logic, and the common law rooted in English history, begotten by the judges and raised on pragmatism. They differ less in detail than in approach. Civil lawyers take a logical approach.

Faced with a legal problem, they turn to the code of jurisdiction, select the appropriate principle and from it deduce the solution. Strong on rationality and theory, they think preferably in terms of rights and duties. Suppose, for instance, that I own a piece of marble and that you make off with it and carve a statue from it: here civil law concerns itself with right of ownership, does the statue belong to the owner of the marble or the sculptor of the statue? The hallmark of common law lawyers is practicality. To solve a legal problem they turn to history, common law principle and judicial precedent, and from these find by trial and error and, if necessary, analogy, an appropriate rule, testing it by its concrete implications. Stronger on pragmatism than logic, they concentrate not on rights, but on remedies. In the marble statue case, common law focuses on the remedies open to the marble owner — restitution or damages. Theory and practice, logic and experience, abstractness and concreteness, generality and particularity are the contrasting features of the civil and common law systems. Both systems are intended to resolve disputes authoritatively according to principles such as certainty, fairness and justice.

It should also be noted that, given its gradual historical development, common law acquired different meanings. In modern day Canada it tends to refer to the laws developed by judges as distinct from statutory laws made by parliament or legislatures, or to the English system of law as opposed to the European civil law system. Historically, common law referred to the law common to the whole of England as distinct from customary local laws. And sometimes it meant the law developed in the common law courts as distinct from that developed in another system of courts that emerged in England, the chancery courts.

This last meaning requires further explanation. The common law was a law of remedies. In order to start a lawsuit it was necessary to obtain a writ, which was an order from the king to the defendant to appear in court to answer a complaint. As a result, the king's clerks influenced the direction of common law. In the thirteenth century, however, influential landowners forced the king to agree not to grant any new kind of writ. From then on a plaintiff could get a writ only if the wrongdoing complained about was one for which a writ had previously been granted. As a result, there were many types of wrong for which the common law could give no remedy. Injured parties who were not covered by the common law turned to the Lord Chancellor, a government minister concerned with equity and justice. A system of equity was developed in the Chancellor's courts to remedy these deficiencies and restrictions. Tensions between the equity and common law courts continued until 1875, when the English Parliament replaced the old courts of common law and equity with a unified high court administering both common law and equity, and laying down that in cases where common law and equity conflict, equity doctrine should prevail. This reintroduced flexibility in the common law. Equity courts never developed to the same degree in colonial settings, and common law proved flexible enough to accommodate to local conditions where there was a conscious effort to avoid a restrictive approach to writs.

As a result of the processes of formal reception, the laws of common law Canadian jurisdictions are not identical to the laws of England. Like equity, ecclesiastical laws never got an authoritative foothold in the colonies. More importantly, after British North American colonies received English law and acquired their own legislative competence to add to and amend the received law, new English laws no longer applied to Canada automatically, although colonial legislation was subject to imperial review and some British legislation was explicitly imperial in reach. Moreover, the decisions of our courts could be appealed to British imperial Judicial Committee of the Privy Council until 1949 and English common law decisions have continued to influence our courts./

During the hundred years between its reception into Nova Scotia (1758) and its reception into the prairie provinces and the territories (1870), common law changed significantly. One factor was the nineteenth century improvement in the quality of law reporting; the better the records, the more the courts relied on them. Another factor affecting this change was the increase in the scale of operations. More judges contributed to the common law in more courts which inevitably resulted in the decline in judicial consensus; during English Chief Justice Mansfield's tenure of office (1756-1788), only 20 dissenting judgments were recorded, whereas today judicial dissent is commonplace. The most important change, however, has been the enormous increase in legislation.

Originally, English statutes, like equity, had been enacted to remedy defects in the common law. As such they had been narrowly construed by courts within the context of the common law in such a way as to minimize their effect on, and alteration of, that law. Acts of Parliament, then, were like isolated islands in a sea of common law. From the late eighteenth century, legislation became the main legal response to the vast changes brought about by the industrial revolution. The courts simply could not keep pace. Moreover, the utilitarian reformers, most notably Jeremy Bentham, rejected the common law tradition as celebrated by William Blackstone earlier in the eighteenth century. Preferring order, logic and rationality to common sense, tradition and history, the utilitarian reformers were influential in giving certain legislative form to vague common law principles. They also argued for the codification of broad areas of law. The situation today is in many respects the reverse of that of 200 years ago: the most important laws and public policies take the form of legislation while common law occupies the gaps left unaddressed by statutes.

To summarize, the historical sources of law in Canada, with the exception of Quebec, are a mixture of:

1. Rules of English common law developed before the date of reception;
2. Rules of English common law developed after this date, because the English courts retained considerable influence and prestige in Canada;
3. Rules of common law developed in Canada;
4. English statutes enacted before the date of reception;
5. British imperial statutes which were possible until the *Statute of Westminster, 1931*[3] and after this date only upon Canada's request and consent until the patriation of the constitution in 1982;
6. Statutes of the federal Parliament of Canada; and
7. Statutes of the provincial assemblies.

With this background in mind we can now turn to some of the more technical aspects of the two main sources of modern Canadian law.

III. THE FORMAL SOURCES OF LAW: LEGISLATION, PRECEDENT AND THEIR APPLICATION

Legal reasoning involves the discerning of the relevant legal rules, their application to a finding of facts, and working out the implications to come up with a decision. While the philosophical and theoretical speculations about the definition and role of law surveyed in Chapter One are important, students studying to be lawyers in professional law school tend to spend most of their time learning the more mundane technical aspects of legal reasoning. This is hardly surprising, especially given the fact that the practical authoritative resolution of disputes by lawyers through negotiation or litigation and judges through adjudication, requires reference to clearly defined and agreed legal rules. We will return to the legal processes of fact-finding in Chapter Five. The practical steps

---

[3]   (U.K.), 22 & 23 Geo. V, c. 4.

of finding law from case reports and legislative sources are introduced in Appendix A. Our concern here is with the two modern sources of law in Canada; how statutes and common law are produced and the basic methods used to discern applicable legal rules from them.

A. Legislation

Legislation is law-making by decree. There are two kinds of legislation: sovereign and subordinate. Sovereign legislation is law made by the authority of Parliament or provincial legislature in accordance with its law-making jurisdiction under the *Constitution Act, 1867*.[4] Subordinate or delegated legislation is law made by a subordinate body given authority by Parliament or provincial legislatures, for instance, the by-laws of a municipality or regulations made by authority of statute.

In Canada, the parameters of sovereign legislative authority are set out in the Constitution Acts, which we will examine in more detail in Chapter Three. Both federal and provincial legislative processes are patterned on the English model dating back to the late medieval and early modern periods. When Parliament emerged it became the rule that a statute would be introduced as a bill, be passed by the House of Commons and the House of Lords and then receive the sovereign's approval before becoming law. At first, Parliament was reluctant to legislate, and earlier statutes merely clarified or consolidated some aspect of the common law. By the end of the seventeenth century, after the turmoil of the English Civil War, the Restoration and the Glorious Revolution, Parliament was clearly established as the supreme law-maker, prevailing over royal prerogative and common law. In Britain and in Commonwealth countries such as Canada, which have preserved parliamentary-style institutions, legislatures sit for the greater part of the year and turn out statutes on every conceivable subject.

How do statutes come into being? A proposal for legislation is introduced as a bill in the House of Commons by a cabinet minister. At this point there is no debate, for this first reading simply informs the House of the proposed legislation. Later, the bill is read a second time and debated as to principle. If approved, it will be sent to a standing committee for detailed study and discussion. If approved in committee, it will be returned to the House, possibly with amendments, for the report stage. It is then read for the third time, and amendments are debated and voted on. If passed, it is then sent to the Senate where the process is repeated. After this, it goes to the Governor General for Royal Assent. Only then does it

---

[4]   (U.K.), 30 & 31 Vict., c. 3, reprinted in R.S.C. 1985, App. II, No. 5.

become a statutory law. Provincial legislatures no longer have an upper house and bills proceed directly from the legislative assembly to the Lieutenant Governor for Royal Assent.

Bills can reflect the implementation of the governing party's political platform or a response to the ongoing demands of government. Only cabinet ministers can introduce bills involving the expenditure of money; otherwise, any member may introduce a bill on any subject. Private members' bills are rare, are mainly introduced to raise an issue, and are allotted a limited number of hours weekly for debate. Unless taken up and supported as government bills, private members' bills are usually talked out and seldom get to a vote. Distinct from private members' bills are private bills, which were customarily introduced in the Senate. These are bills that confer rights on, or relieve from liability, a particular person or body of persons. Many of these "persons" are corporate in nature, and include charities and universities. Historically, couples seeking divorce would have to obtain a private bill.

Statutes, acts, or legislation, then, are formal expressions of the will of Parliament or provincial legislatures. They are a manifestation of public policy given in the form of law in order to manage areas seen to be of pressing public importance. Judges play an important role in giving statutes practical application.

However, this formal expression of public policy may prove difficult to interpret. First, the legislature may not have foreseen the exact circumstances the court has to deal with. Try as they might, governments will never be able to draft provisions that anticipate all the different disputes and fact situations that might come before the courts. There is a tension between the generality of statutory words and specificity of real situations that judges must resolve. Second, language is not as immune from interpretive differences as fields like mathematics; meanings depend upon context, and words mean different things to different people. Sometimes, judges may harbour doubts about the reach of public policy or jealously guard their own law-making authority, which they see as being threatened by the statute. Language is malleable and is given meaning in accordance with the values of the person interpreting it.

How then do the courts determine what the legislature actually meant?

Those who study statutory interpretation identify three basic patterns or approaches; the literal, golden and mischief rules:

1. THE LITERAL RULE

This tends to be the approach most judges favour in most circumstances. This holds that the words in a statute be given their plain and ordinary meaning. As Lord Chief Justice Tindall declared in *Sussex Peerage Case*:[5]

> The only rule for the construction of Acts of Parliament is that they should be construed according to the intent of the Parliament which passed the Act. If the words of the statute are in themselves precise and unambiguous, then no more can be necessary than to expound those words in their natural ordinary sense. The words themselves alone do, in such case, best declare the intention of the lawgiver.

Some argue that the literal rule is in keeping with the doctrine that Parliament or the provincial legislatures are the supreme law-makers and that the courts should not legislate under the guise of interpretation. In other situations, however, literal interpretation allows the judge to decide that the legislation does not cover the situation at hand.

2. THE GOLDEN RULE

This rule (as spelled out *Grey v. Pearson*[6]) requires words in a statute to be given their plain and ordinary grammatical meaning unless this would lead to such absurdity, inconsistency or inconvenience that Parliament could not have intended it. The law can be modified so far as to avoid absurdity. This approach has now mostly fallen into disuse, departure from the literal rule being only justified today by inconsistency between different provisions of a statute or between provisions in two or more statutes. Both the literal and golden rules allow judges to narrow the applicability of statutes.

3. THE MISCHIEF RULE

This rule allows judges to consider the underlying purpose of the legislation, the "mischief" government was seeking to address when the legislation was originally passed. To paraphrase a description of this approach in *Heydon's Case*:[7]

1.   What was the common law before the making of the Act?
2.   What was the mischief and defect for which the common law did not provide?

---

[5]   [1844] All E.R. Rep. 55 at 63.
[6]   (1857), 10 E.R. 1216 (H.L.).
[7]   (1584), 76 E.R. 637.

3.   What remedy did Parliament resolve?
4.   What was the reason for the remedy, and how best can the court suppress the mischief and advance the remedy?

In searching for the underlying object of the legislation, courts in Canada and Britain, unlike in the United States, do not consider legislative history, parliamentary debates, government pronouncements or press reports about what politicians said about the law. The courts are beginning to relax this rule somewhat by referring to official documents such as the reports of Royal Commissions and Legislative Committees. Generally, the mischief rule is adopted if the judge wishes to widen the applicability of legislation.

Finally, it should be noted that there are certain other matters which may be taken into account in interpreting a statute. First, the words in question may have been defined by an interpretation section in the statute. Second, they may have been defined in a general Interpretation Act. Both federal Parliament and the provinces have passed such acts defining many commonly used words and generally directing judges to interpret enactments as remedial and to give them a liberal construction that best ensures the attainment of their objects. Finally, statutes are interpreted in the light of other statutes on the same subject and in the context of the common law, which includes various presumptions developed over time by the courts. Unless it expressly stated the contrary, legislation is not to be interpreted in such a way as to fundamentally change the common law.

Statutory interpretation, then, is not a simple and straightforward matter of applying legislative words to different fact situations. Sometimes words may be clear and precise enough to be construed without any difficulty. Often enough, however, they may be sufficiently ambiguous to give rise to conflicting interpretations. In such cases the judges have recourse to any or all of the three rules of interpretation, or to numerous other considerations.

B. Precedent

The other main source of law in Canada derives from precedents or cases that make up the common law. To find the law on issues not covered by statutes, we turn to the decisions of the courts, and to arrive at these decisions, the courts themselves have had recourse to previous decisions. Common law is judge-made law based on precedents. It fills the gaps left unaddressed by legislation.

Doing what we have always done is natural; we save time and trouble and avoid putting every question to an agonizing reappraisal. It makes life more certain and predictable — we can more easily foresee what people are going to do. Consequently, it also makes for fairness and consistency; like cases are treated alike and different cases differently. Following precedent, then, is in no way unusual. Fairness and consistency after all are important aspects of justice. As we saw in the last section, common law originated with the practice of sending royal judges throughout the realm of England to oversee the administration of the different regions and to try serious crimes and disputes. The judges naturally tended to give similar decisions in similar cases, and being relatively few in number, knew one another so well that each judge was quite familiar with the other's practice. There was, accordingly, a kind of judicial consensus as to the common law. By the eighteenth century, however, with industrialization and rapid urbanization, life was growing ever more complex. More laws and more judges were necessary. The growth of statutes was one consequence, as we have seen. As well, the greater number of judges meant more difficulties in reaching consensus about the law. Without first-hand knowledge of their peers' practices and decisions, judges had to rely on reported cases. Hence the importance of law reports, the respect for authority and the significance of a single decision enshrined in a leading case. Accordingly, it has been said, the history of the common law is the story of a journey from principle to precedent.

Judicial precedents are central to the operation of the modern common law, where courts not only follow previous customary practices but also single previous decisions. They operate according to a doctrine called *stare decisis*. Under this doctrine, there are two types of precedent: binding and persuasive precedents. A binding precedent is one that a court has to follow. A persuasive precedent is one that a court may take into account. The court does not have to follow the persuasive precedent but very often will because the court feels it should be followed.

Which category a precedent falls into depends on two factors: (1) what courts bind other courts, and (2) what a case is actually authority for. The first factor is related to court hierarchy: which court does the precedent come from? *Stare decisis* holds that like cases must be decided alike if there is a precedent by a higher court within the court's jurisdiction. It also holds that like cases may be decided alike if there is a precedent at the same level of court or outside the court's jurisdiction. The second factor is about identifying the core principles and characteristics that decide the precedent case. To elaborate:

WHICH COURTS BIND OTHER COURTS?

Basically there are two simple rules. First, higher courts bind lower courts and not vice versa. The Supreme Court of Canada decisions bind the Ontario Court of Appeal, for example, but the Ontario Court of Appeal decisions do not bind the Supreme Court of Canada. Second, courts are not bound by courts of a different jurisdiction or by courts of equal status. The Ontario courts are not bound by, say, the Manitoba Court of Appeal because Ontario and Manitoba are two different jurisdictions. All courts, however, are bound by the Supreme Court of Canada, which has jurisdiction throughout the country. Decisions, whether from another province, from England or some other common law jurisdiction such as Australia, may be referred to as persuasive authority. However, English decisions are particularly important for two reasons. First, all English decisions reached prior to the date of formal reception are binding unless that law has subsequently been changed. Second, for many years after reception, decisions of the English courts were so prestigious as to be generally regarded as binding in Canada and they continue to receive more attention than decisions of other common law jurisdictions outside of Canada.

Courts are not bound by courts of equal jurisdiction but they will naturally respect previous decisions as persuasive authority. What about the highest courts? Until 1959, the Supreme Court of Canada saw itself as bound by the decisions not only by the British Judicial Committee of the Privy Council (JCPC) (ten years after appeals to the JCPC were abolished) but also the English House of Lords, the highest appeal court in England. In 1966, the House of Lords itself declared it was no longer bound by its own prior decisions, and in 1975 the Supreme Court of Canada declared it was no longer bound by its own decisions.

WHAT DO PRECEDENT CASES ACTUALLY STAND FOR?

When a court is bound by a previous decision, what precisely is it bound by? What is a previous case authority for and what does it decide? It is not the entire case report that binds. The core legal principle decides the case, what is called the *ratio decidendi*, which serves as the precedent. The court will decide matters of law, questions of fact and remedies between the parties to a dispute. So, if Smith goes to court for an injunction to stop a neighbour, Brown, from making excessive noise, the court's judgment will decide whether Brown is making noise (a question of fact), whether this constitutes a nuisance (a question of law), and whether Smith shall get an injunction (a question concerning remedies). Smith and Brown are absolutely bound by these decisions, and although they can appeal against them to a higher court, they cannot raise them in another case before another trial court (the doctrine of *res judicata*). The only aspect in *Smith v. Brown* that is binding as a precedent is the court's decision on the legal question of what constitutes a nuisance. This core legal principle is what lawyers call the *ratio decidendi* of the case. The rest of the decision is termed *obiter dicta.*

There are three aspects to identifying the *ratio decidendi*. First, it is the point of law raised by the case and decided by the judge. In other words, the *ratio decidendi* is the rule of law that the judge formulates or uses to come to the decision, not some point of law mentioned in the course of argument but not raised by the case. Second, how is it found? In early cases, the reports did not set out an explicit rule and it must be inferred from the issue between the parties and the factual circumstances of the particular case. Finally, what is a case authority for? This is the most difficult apsect of the doctrine of *stare decisis*. Unpopular decisions may be avoided by drawing a distinction between the precedent case and the case being decided. Conversely, with popular decisions we may find the opposite. Accordingly, to know what a case is authority for, we have to trace its subsequent history. Has it been extended? Has it been distinguished? Has it been over-ruled by later decisions in higher courts? Or has it been swept aside by statute? The authority of a precedent is never fixed, the law is always evolving.

From this review it is apparent that there are some large variables in the operation of precedent in common law. It involves reasoning by example: does the case at hand sufficiently resemble the precedent case in its relevant aspects. Judges who wish not to be bound by a percedent may distinguish some aspect of the case at hand from the precedent case. Identification of *ratio decidendi* is fraught with different possibilities of interpretation. What is the central deciding principle? Is there more than one guiding principle? Are the principles to be interpreted narrowly or widely? There is considerable range for subjective choice. If judges wish to be bound by a precedent they will emphasize the similarities, if not, they will highlight the differences.

As the sceptical and critical legal scholars introduced in Chapter One point out, despite the practical authoritative requirements of dispute resolution, appearances of objectivity in the processes of law discernment and application are deceptive. While there are constraints of logic, consistency, and the obvious need to justify decisions by legal authority, there are also more subjective considerations at play. What result best accords with the judge's own sense of justice? What result accords with the judge's perceptions of good public policy and other values? Judges tend to be more constrained with statutory sources of law than they are with common law, but as we have seen there is considerable room for difference in the interpretation and application of legislation. Sometimes judges may harbour doubts about the reach of public policy or attempt to guard what they consider to be the proper law-making authority vested in the judiciary. From this perspective, statutes intrude on the exercise of necessary judicial discretion.

Which is the better way of making law, precedent or legislation? Much can be said in favour of both methods. Precedent is gradual whereas legislation can dramatically transform the state's approach to problems. Precedent is made after consideration of the arguments put forward by the parties affected and pragmatically addresses issues particular to individual disputes. Legislators can take a much wider view, considering all sorts of evidence and views gathered in committees or commissions and pass comprehensive statutes. Precedent is retrospective and relates to situations arising prior to the decision, while legislation can be prospective and lay down new rules beforehand. Finally, precedent is made by judges appointed to office based on their experience in the law, while legislation is made by democratically elected representatives.

Judicial and legislative processes are by no means perfect ways of law-making. There are advantages and disadvantages to both. Historical experience in Canada also suggests that both these sources of current formal law reflect the imposition of one powerful culture over less powerful ones. How Canada received its law is bound up with conquest and colonization. Our legal system was not introduced into a vacuum, nor did it involve much in the way of consensus or inherent legal superiority. The experiences of our first nations and the influence of civil law systems world-wide make this clear.

FURTHER READING

J.E. Coté, "The Reception of English Law" (1977), 15 Alberta Law Review 46

E.A. Driedger, *The Construction of Statutes* (Scarborough: Butterworths, 1983)

J.Y. Henderson, "The Doctrine of Aboriginal Rights" in M. Boldt & J.A. Long eds., *The Quest for Justice: Aboriginal Peoples and Aboriginal Rights* (Toronto: University of Toronto Press, 1985) at 185

B. Laskin, The British Tradition in Canadian Law (London: Stevens, 1969).

M.R. McGuigan, "Precedent and Policy in the Supreme Court" (1967), 45 Canadian Bar Review 627

B.W. Morse ed., *Aboriginal Peoples and the Law: Indian, Metis and Inuit Rights in Canada* (Ottawa: Carleton University Press, 1985)

M.H. Ogilvie, *Historical Introduction to Legal Studies* (Toronto: Carswell, 1982)

W. Twining & D. Miers, *How to Do Things with Rules* (London: Weidenfeld & Nicolson, 1982)

G. Williams, *Learning the Law* (London: Stevens, 1982)

J. Willis, "Statute Interpretation in a Nutshell" (1938), 14 Canadian Bar Review 1

Chapter Three

The Canadian Constitution

A state is an organized political community with a government and territory. The constitution is the set of rules defining its organization and operation. Such constitutional rules are found in every state, and are considered by many to be the most fundamental formal rules because they regulate the state itself. As we will see, the constitutional rules are made up of customs, conventions and laws about the different institutions of the state, their composition and powers, and their relationships with one another and with citizens.

Not all states have the same kind of constitution. Some, like the United States, have put their constitutional rules into one basic document. Other states, including the United Kingdom, have no such single document, and their constitutions are described as "unwritten constitutions". This is so, even though the United Kingdom does have several important documents like the *Magna Carta*, the *Bill of Rights* and the *Act of Settlement*, that contain provisions that we might describe as written constitutional elements. Constitutions of the former type (*i.e.*, those contained in a single document) are often referred to as written constitutions.

Another constitutional classification is a distinction drawn between "flexible" and "rigid" constitutions. According to A.V. Dicey, the nineteenth century English constitutional scholar introduced in Chapter One, a flexible constitution is one under which every law can legally be changed with the same ease and in the same manner by the sovereign authority. A rigid constitution is one in which certain fundamental constitutional laws cannot be changed in the same manner as ordinary laws. A flexible constitution can be simply amended, whereas a rigid constitution can only be amended through special procedures. For example, British constitutional amendments are relatively simply achieved through parliamentary statutes. Amendments of the United States Constitution require a two thirds vote of both Houses of Congress and ratification by the legislatures of three-fourths of the states, or initiation by two-thirds of the states and ratification by conventions in three-quarters of the states.

How should we classify the Canadian constitution? In many respects it falls between the written and unwritten models. Since 1867, the basic constitutional rules prevailing in the United Kingdom have been the foundation of Canada's constitution. These include everything from the institutional relationship between Parliament, the courts and the Crown, to the minute details of parliamentary procedure. However, unlike the United Kingdom, Canada also has specific basic constitutional enactments. Some of these serve to regulate the composition and operation of a system of multiple legislative authority. Others include an explicit enumeration of constitutional rights enforceable by the courts. Still others specify processes for future constitutional amendment. Unlike the position in the United States, these enactments are not set out in a single document but several: the *Canada Act 1982* and *Constitution Act, 1982*, and 24 other Acts and orders, mostly comprising the Constitution Acts 1867-1975 (formerly the British North America Acts 1867-1975).

The Canadian constitution also falls between the flexible and rigid models. It is a mixture of parliamentary supremacy and substantive checks on unfettered legislative powers. No special procedures are required to alter laws not contained in the basic constitutional documents. Legislative practices or federal and provincial statutes on human rights, for example, can be readily altered by majority governments acting within their jurisdiction. Despite this flexibility, however, the Canadian constitution has some rigid elements; for example legislatures cannot pass laws outside their constitutionally defined jurisdiction. In addition, the *Charter of Rights and Freedoms* gives judges the power to consider the validity of statutes and the exercise of public authority, such that the exercise of legislative power is always potentially subject to the process of judicial review. Finally, amendment of our constitutional arrangements requires resort to processes that go beyond the exercise of ordinary legislative processes. These are constitutional checks that limit the powers of Parliament and provincial legislatures.

Today, a constitution tends to be regarded as a badge of nationhood. As such, it may reflect the values that a country regards as important and show how they are to be protected. In Canada, these values are manifested in constitutional features such as the vesting of law-making authority into the hands of democratically elected representatives, the non-partisan administration of law and certain executive functions of the state, and a charter of rights.

These features of our constitution have developed through an evolution to self-government from colonial status. In this respect, we share experiences with countries such as Australia and New Zealand. We also stand in contrast to countries such as the United States and France, where constitutions were formed relatively quickly through a revolutionary experience.

Some argue that a kind of colonialism still prevails in the relations between the central Canadian state and peoples who regard themselves as sovereign within the territory of our country. Can the aspirations of French Canada be accommodated through measures of official bilingualism and the provincial status of Quebec? What about the aspirations of aboriginal peoples who assumed that their nationhood would be respected through treaties? These formidable constitutional challenges mean that Canada may face fundamental constitutional change in the future.

The national ideals set out in a constitution sometimes stand in remarkable variance with the prevailing reality in a state. The constitutions of the Soviet Union, for instance, contained extensive declarations of rights and principles for the liberation of individuals and social groups. High-sounding constitutions are of little value unless both the government and the people recognize its legitimacy, consent to abide by it and strive to ensure the maintenance of its principles. What is written on paper, said Montesquieu in the eighteenth century, is less important than "that which is graven on the hearts of men."

I. THE BRITISH CONSTITUTIONAL BASIS

In the preamble of the *Constitution Act, 1867*[1] (formerly the *British North America Act, 1867*), we read that the four founding provinces wished to be "federally united into one Dominion" with a constitution "similar in principle to that of the United Kingdom." We will examine the implications of the federal union, Confederation, in the next section. First, we need to explore the British constitutional principles that form the basis of our constitution.

The constitution of the United Kingdom is characterized by the "rule of law", which is supported by two related features concerning the operation of the courts and legislatures. These two features are judicial independence and parliamentary sovereignty as exercised through responsible government. Each of these aspects of the British constitution will be considered in turn with reference to their implications for Canada.

---

[1] (U.K.), 30 & 31 Vict., c. 3, reprinted in R.S.C. 1985, App. II, No. 5.

A. The Rule of Law

The first basic feature of the United Kingdom constitution is the rule of law. According to the constitutional scholar A.V. Dicey, rule of law involves two aspects. First, law is supreme over all other expressions of power. Law prevails over the exercise of arbitrary, executive or discretionary forms of authority. Second, no one is above the law, and everyone is equal before the law. Even the most high-ranking government officials are not exempt from duties imposed on ordinary citizens.

An illustration of the application of rule of law in Canada is the case of *Roncarelli v. Duplessis.*[2] The defendant's position as Premier of Quebec did not prevent him from being held liable in damages for acting arbitrarily. Roncarelli was a Jehovah's Witness and often put up bail for fellow members of that sect who were being harassed by public officials in Quebec on account of their beliefs. In 1946, Roncarelli had his liquor licence cancelled at the instigation of Premier Duplessis, who was also Attorney General of the province. The Supreme Court of Canada found that Duplessis acted outside his jurisdiction in a private capacity and awarded Roncarelli damages. Justice Rand stated that, "in public regulation of this sort there is no such thing as absolute and untrammeled 'discretion'" and Justice Abbott declared, "the executive branch of government does not make the law but merely carries it out or administers it."

The root idea behind the rule of law is that the government must be restricted to doing only such acts as are authorized by law. This purpose is thwarted if the government can change the law at will to suit itself. In order for the rule of law to work effectively, the laws must be correctly generated by duly constituted authority and they must be administered by an impartial authority.

The doctrine of the separation of powers attempts to achieve these objectives. According to this doctrine the three basic areas of state power must be distributed to separate and independent institutions. The power of governing, administering and enforcing the laws should belong to the executive. The power of making, altering and repealing the laws should belong to the legislature. And the power of adjudicating on disputes according to law, including disputes about the exercise of executive and legislative powers, should belong to an independent judiciary. We begin with the last of these.

---

[2] [1959] S.C.R. 2.

B. Judicial Independence

As some constitutional experts argue, the rule of law may appear to be inconsistent with parliamentary supremacy. How is it, for example, that Parliament, in exercising its law-making function, can be considered to be supreme if the rule of law holds that the law itself is supreme over all other expressions of power. According to Dicey, this ambiguity or problem is resolved through the idea of judicial independence. Judges perform a vital function in reconciling the rule of law and the supremacy of Parliament. They do this through their review of the validity of statutes passed by Parliament, which are expressions of Parliament's will and law-making powers. Dicey holds that the will of Parliament can be expressed only in the form of an act, the application of which must be ultimately interpreted as valid, or remedied if invalid, by the courts. The formal guarantees of judicial independence or impartiality that evolved through British constitutional history were "security of tenure" and an institutional development of the "separation of powers" doctrine.

After the *Act of Settlement, 1701*, judges in Britain no longer held their office according to royal pleasure. Judges could not be dismissed if their rulings displeased the sovereign or government cabinets. Instead judges held office on the basis of good behaviour. They could be dismissed only if their behaviour on the bench was found wanting by a resolution of both houses of Parliament. This security of tenure was adopted in Canada in 1867.

The practical extension of separation of powers doctrine to the judiciary was achieved in 1803 when the British government agreed to exclude leading judges from government cabinets. This practice was adopted in the Canadian provinces in the 1830s and 1840s and was entrenched by the time of confederation.

Do these formal protections of judicial independence guarantee impartial courts? They do not address how judges are appointed in the first place and how their values impact on their decisions. Judges venture into public policy when they review the actions of the state or are asked to weigh the balance to be struck between individual rights and public interests in legislation. How much impact judges should have on such decidedly political matters in the court and how much they should be able to talk about such matters outside of court are contentious matters in present day Canada. We explore these issues at greater length in Chapter Seven.

C. Parliamentary Sovereignty and Responsible Government

The doctrine of separation of powers also segregates the authority of the legislature and the executive. The relationship between executive and legislative institutions, as they have developed in British constitutional history, form the other basis for the effective operation of the rule of law. Not only must laws be administered by impartial courts, the laws themselves must be correctly generated by duly constituted authority. This other practical requirement for the rule of law involves parliamentary sovereignty and responsible government.

The medieval powers of the Crown or executive authority in England were eventually checked by the *Magna Carta*. Executive powers grew again under the reign of the Tudors prior to the start of the seventeenth century, and political tensions eventually culminated in the English Civil War, the execution of King Charles I, and temporary rule by Cromwell's Commonwealth Parliament during the mid-1600s. The restoration of the monarchy eventually led to the constitutional equilibrium achieved with the Glorious Revolution of 1689, which was accompanied by important libertarian legislation such as the *Bill of Rights*, the *Habeas Corpus Act*, the *Treason Act* and the *Act of Settlement*. Together, these measures established Parliament as the supreme law-maker, limited the prerogatives of the Crown and established procedural rights that limited governments' legal powers against individuals.

However, throughout the eighteenth century, the practice of appointing ministers and forming cabinents continued at the behest of the King. Moreover, the democratic franchise to elect members of Parliament was limited and the idea of a loyal opposition party had yet to gain full legitimacy. It was only with the political struggles of the late eighteenth and early nineteenth centuries that the modern features of parliamentary democracy took shape. In Canada, responsible cabinet government, or cabinets formed by members of the majority party in the elected house and directly answerable to it, was only achieved after much conflict in 1849.

In Canada, as in Britain, the government of the day is formed by the leader of the political party that elects the most members to the legislature (the House of Commons or a provincial assembly). Responsible government means that the government has to respond to political issues through the relevant government minister. Ministers are answerable to the House of Commons or the provincial legislature, as the case may be, and the representatives in these bodies are in turn answerable to the electorate. Under the Canadian parliamentary system, and unlike what happens in the United States, government ministers are not kept separate and apart from the legislature but sit as members of one of the houses of Parliament.

While responsible government puts governments under the direct authority of the elected legislators the accountability achieved often turns out to be a "paper tiger". Governments, by controlling their own members, can control legislatures and can indirectly make and unmake laws as they please.

Britain's basic constitutional rule, as noted earlier, is that Parliament can make or unmake any law. "Parliament", is said, "can do anything but make a man or woman." To which it is replied that it could do this too, for if Parliament decreed that men were women, then for legal purposes they would be. For legal purposes, then (subject to the role of an independent judiciary in resolving tensions between the idea of parliamentary supremacy and the rule of law), Parliament is absolutely sovereign. It can make, amend or repeal what laws it likes. The *Magna Carta*, the *Bill of Rights*, the *Habeas Corpus Act*, the *Act of Settlement* and any other fundamental constitutional statutes can theoretically be set aside by ordinary legislation in the United Kingdom.

This absolute sovereignty of the elected Parliament is, of course, subject to the demands of political reality. For instance, it is unlikely that the British Parliament can repeal acts such as the *Statute of Westminster, 1931*[3] and the *Canada Act 1982*,[4] which were requested by governments of former colonies to enhance their self-government. The ultimate accountability of elected representatives to the ballot box means that laws that limit Parliament's omnipotence in other areas could not be easily repealed.

However, questions remain whether political realities facing governments are a sufficient check on the legislative sovereignty of Parliament. The basic principle that Parliament can make any law it likes needs to be qualified, arguably, by fundamental laws that lie beyond the reach of Parliament. In Canada such fundamental laws, which Parliament or the provincial assemblies cannot unilaterally amend, are in fact found in the written aspects of our constitution, notably the Constitution Acts, 1867 and 1982.

The written aspects of the Canadian constitution check parliamentary supremacy in three ways. First, the federal system established in 1867 distributes powers between the federal government and the provinces in such a way that each is sovereign within its proper jurisdiction, not outside it.

---

[3] (U.K.), 22 & 23 Geo. V, c. 4.

[4] (U.K.), 1982, c. 11.

Second, until 1982, the Canadian Parliament and provincial legislatures could not amend basic constitutional arrangements without legislation first being passed in the British House of Commons. Since 1982 and the patriation of the constitution, domestic constitutional amending formulas must be followed. Third, federal and the provincial laws are subject to the fundamental rules set out in the *Canadian Charter of Rights and Freedoms*.

II. THE CANADIAN CONSTITUTIONAL CONTENT

As we saw in Chapter Two, British settlement of what we now know as Canada introduced English common law and statutes, a system of English style courts and representative legislatures. Each British North American colonial legislature could pass new laws in relation to their own provincial jurisdiction. However, the exercise of this power was subject to British review by the Colonial Office, imperial statutes intended to apply to them could still be passed by the British Parliament, and the appeal of court decisions were heard by the British Judicial Committee of the Privy Council. After the achievement of responsible government Canadian jurisdictions nonetheless became increasingly self-governing.

The powers of self-governing colonies were formalized in the *Colonial Laws Validity Act, 1865*,[5] which laid down that (1) self-governing colonies could enact valid legislation provided it was not inconsistent with "imperial legislation", (*i.e.*, legislation meant to apply throughout the British Empire) and (2) the United Kingdom Parliament could still legislate for such self-governing colonies. Two years later, in accordance with that Act and the request of the existing provincial governments, the British Parliament passed the *British North America Act, 1867*.[6] This Act established the confederation of Canada, set up the institutions of federation and distributed legislative powers between the new Dominion government in Ottawa and the provinces. As an imperial statute, the *British North America Act* could not be altered in Canada.

The subsequent steps toward self-government involved greater autonomy of British dominions such as Canada, Australia and New Zealand from Britain in areas such as international relations. These steps were accelerated by experiences such as the First World War. Following the war the affair known as the "King-Byng controversy" caused a crisis concerning Canadian sovereignty and the powers of the Governor General

---

[5]   (U.K.), 28 & 29 Vict., c. 63.
[6]   (U.K.), 30 & 31 Vict., c. 3, reprinted in R.S.C. 1985, App. II, No. 5.

(Crown's representative in Canada). The Governor General, Lord Byng refused the Prime Minister Mackenzie-King's request to dissolve Parliament for a general election and instead asked Conservative leader Arthur Meighen to form the government. In the same year (1926), the Judicial Committee of the Privy Council struck down federal legislation abolishing criminal appeals to the council. These events, among others, led the dominions to lobby for yet more autonomy. The *Statute of Westminster, 1931* conferred even greater independence. Agreement was reached that (1) Britain could legislate for a dominion only at its request and consent and could not strike down dominion legislation, and (2) the dominion could repeal any English statute, imperial or otherwise. In effect, further British legislative intervention was precluded.

An exception remained in the case of constitutional amendment however. At Canada's request, pending agreement in Canada on an amending formula for the *British North America Act*, a restriction was made to prevent repeal or alteration of that Imperial Act in Canada. After 1931, numerous minor amendments to the *British North America Act* were made at Canada's request by the British Parliament. Able to amend some provisions related to their own powers through requests to the British Parliament, provincial and federal governments focused on issues where jurisdictions overlapped. Conflicts over legislative enactments that raised jurisdictional questions between the two levels of government were taken up in appeals to the Judicial Committee of the Privy Council.

The intervention of British courts continued until appeals to the Judicial Committee of the Privy Council were abolished in 1949, at which time the Supreme Court of Canada became the country's final court of appeal. However, the matter of constitutional amendment remained unresolved. While the federal government introduced a Bill of Rights in 1960, it was not entrenched as part of the constitution and it remained difficult to get consensus between the provincial and federal governments on more fundamental constitutional change. Finally, in 1982 the Canadian constitution was "patriated". To accomplish this, the Canadian Parliament submitted a request to the British Parliament for a large package of constitutional legislation. The submission had the agreement of all provinces except Quebec, and had been supported by a constitutional reference opinion by the Supreme Court of Canada prepared on the request of the federal government. The package included provisions that gave Canada full power to amend its constitution without reference to the British Parliament, and provided for the constitutional entrenchment of the Charter. The British Parliament passed the *Canada Act 1982*[7] and it was proclaimed by Queen Elizabeth in Ottawa on April 17, 1982.

The *Canada Act* specifies that the *Constitution Act, 1982*,[8] shall be law in Canada and that no Act enacted subsequently by the British Parliament shall apply to Canada. The *Constitution Act, 1982* (see Appendix Three) itself contains two large additions to Canadian constitutional law; the *Canadian Charter of Rights and Freedoms*[9] and a formula setting out procedures for the future amendments to the Canadian constitution. It also contains procedures for the amendment of the *British North America Act* henceforth to be known as the *Constitution Act, 1867* (also see Appendix Three) and provisions that attempt to give constitutional recognition to federal/provincial conferences, the rights of aboriginal peoples and the equalization of regional disparities. Section 52 of the *Constitution Act, 1982* sums matters up by enumerating Canada's various constitutional statutes, stating that the Canadian constitution is made up of:

1. The *Canada Act 1982* and *Constitution Act, 1982*;
2. The 24 other Acts and Orders noted in Schedule 1 of the Act, mostly comprising the Constitution Acts 1867-1975 (formerly the BNA Acts 1867-1975); and
3. Any amendments to 1 and 2.

These constitutional changes have created new procedures for amending the constitution of Canada and have constitutionally entrenched the Charter, considerably extending the powers of the judiciary in a manner that further restricts legislative powers. We will not examine domestic attempts to further amend the constitution since 1982, apart from observing that there has not been a great deal of success as evidenced by the failure of the Meech Lake and Charlottetown Accords. Our focus here is on the two main aspects of Canadian constitutional law that limit legislative powers and supplement or provide the "Canadian content" to our British constitutional foundation. These are federalism and the *Canadian Charter of Rights and Freedoms*.

---

[7] (U.K.), 1982, c. 11.

[8] Being Schedule B to the *Canada Act 1982* (U.K.), 1982, c. 11.

[9] Part I of the *Constitution Act, 1982* being Schedule B to the *Canada Act 1982* (U.K.), 1982, c. 11.

A. Federalism

The United Kingdom is a unitary state, meaning that all power to make statute law is vested in one parliamentary body (although limited legislative powers are currently being "devolved" to new assemblies in Scotland, Northern Ireland and Wales). Canada, like Australia and the United States, is a long-established federal state. Since the Dominion of Canada came into existence in 1867, legislative authority has been divided between the federal and provincial governments, each level having discrete jurisdictions. Compared with unitary systems, our system, with its federal laws and ten different sets of provincial laws and three different sets of territorial laws, is extremely complex. This complexity lies beyond the scope of this chapter. However, some general observations can be made about the division of powers and the role of judicial review of the exercise of legislative powers.

The essence of a federation is that citizens are ruled partly by the central government and partly by the government of their province. This means two things. First, powers must be divided between the two levels of government. Second, the legal principles on which such division is based must put it beyond the power of either level of government to usurp the authority of the other. In Canada this is achieved by sections 91 and 92 of the *Constitution Act, 1867*. Section 91 defines the main powers and authority of the Canadian Parliament, and applies to areas such as national defence, trade and commerce, international relations, and criminal law. Section 92 sets out the main provincial powers such as property and civil matters, municipalities, and the enforcement of criminal law. Residual powers, that is, the power to pass laws not expressly reserved to the provinces under section 92, fall to the federal government and its jurisdiction over laws that relate to the "Peace, Order and good Government" of Canada. The complex division of responsibilities for the courts and the appointment of judges is examined in Chapters Six and Seven.

The main role of our courts in constitutional matters, at least until the adoption of the Charter in 1982, was to resolve disputes between different levels of government over jurisdiction. The division of legislative powers, determining who has power over what, cannot be adequately understood by simply reading sections 91 and 92 of the *Constitution Act, 1867*. The dual enumeration of powers provides great potential for overlap and all the modern issues that concern government and require a legislative response could not possibly be anticipated in 1867. In order to fully understand the divisions of legislative powers in Canada one has to go to the cases that interpret the provisions.

Generally, neither level of government can encroach, or trench, as lawyers put it, on the law-making authority of the other. Two examples illustrate this point. In *Switzman v. Elbling*,[10] a Quebec statute outlawing propagation of communism (the *Act Respecting Communistic Propaganda*[11] or the "Padlock" Act) was held invalid, not because it curtailed freedom of speech, but because it attempted to enact criminal law, a matter exclusively within federal jurisdiction. Conversely, in the *Re Board of Commerce Act*,[12] a federal statute prohibiting hoarding was held invalid, not because it interfered with liberty, but because it sought to regulate use of property, a matter exclusively for provincial jurisdiction.

Provincial governments battled the federal government in the courts over jurisdictional power and many commentators suggest that the provinces won most of them. Judicial review in federalism disputes tended to have a decentralizing effect. Section 92 powers were usually interpreted widely and section 91 powers narrowly, despite the fact that the federal government had residual powers. Many of the important precedents that established this general tendency were reached by the Judicial Committee of the Privy Council (JCPC). After appeals to this court were ended the Supreme Court of Canada tended to defer to these decisions.

Some argue that this decentralizing pattern accommodated Canada's growing diversity. Others suggest that the JCPC decisions were a disguise for imperialism; that by limiting federal powers and enhancing provincial powers, Britain sought to maximize its influence and limit Canada's independence. There is little question that the provinces had very effective advocates such as Ontario Attorney General and Premier Oliver Mowatt. They argued that confederation was a compact between self-governing provinces under threat by a growing central state in Ottawa.

B. The Charter of Rights

The *Canadian Charter of Rights and Freedoms*, which accompanied the patriation of the constitution in 1982, creates an additional major role for courts in constitutional matters. It is a new role that has received a great deal of attention, as well as controversy, over the past two decades.

As is evident from what we have surveyed thus far, the Charter is only one part of the Canadian constitution. Moreover, Canadians did not suddenly acquire rights in 1982 that did not exist before. The reception of English constitutional liberties, the introduction of federalism, and the *Bill of Rights, 1960* all provided symbolic and indirect limits on state powers over individual rights. However, courts were not

---

10 [1957] S.C.R. 285.
11 R.S.Q. 1941, c. 52.
12 [1922] A.C. 191.

obliged to consider alleged rights violations and could not invalidate legislation or other state actions as unconstitutional. The Charter has opened up the means for citizens to challenge the state. This has extended the role of the courts in protecting individual rights and enhanced their role in Canadian public policy. This creates a new check on the powers of Parliament and the legislatures. For this reason, the Charter receives the lion's share of attention in current debates about Canadian constitutional law.

The Charter is constitutionally entrenched and overriding. It cannot be amended or repealed by ordinary legislation but only by the special procedures set out in the *Constitution Act, 1982* itself (if Parliament as well as seven provinces representing at least 50 per cent of the population are in agreement). Unlike the *Canadian Bill of Rights*, which applied only to federal legislation, it applies to all levels of government, obliging them to conform to Charter rights through judicial review.

Many of the early Charter judgements discussed principles of interpretation. Echoing the JCPC in its interpretation of the *British North America Act*, the courts noted that as a constitutional document, the Charter should be given a liberal interpretation. Brian Dickson, the first Charter era Chief Justice of the Supreme Court of Canada, stated that the Charter should be "capable of growth and development over time to meet new social, political and historical realities often unimagined by its framers." This is a far cry from the situation under the *Canadian Bill of Rights*, in which the same court adopted narrow interpretations of rights.

1. RIGHTS UNDER THE CHARTER

The rights as set out in the Charter fall into several categories:

1.   Fundamental Freedoms (*e.g.*, freedom of conscience, belief, expression, peaceful assembly and association);
2.   Democratic Rights (*e.g.*, the right to vote, to run for political office, the sitting of elected representative institutions and their duration during war and emergencies);
3.   Mobility Rights (*e.g.*, the right to enter, remain in and leave Canada and to reside and work in any part of the country);
4.   Legal Rights (*e.g.*, the right not to be deprived of liberty and security, not to be subject to unreasonable search and seizure of the person, rights on criminal charges, arrest and detention);
5.   Equality Rights (*e.g.*, the right to be treated equally without discrimination);

6.   Language Rights (*e.g.*, the equality of status of the English and French languages with respect their use in all institutions of the Parliament and Government of Canada); and
7.   Minority Language Education Rights (*e.g.*, the right of English speaking Canadians who reside in the province of Quebec to have their children educated in English).

The Charter contains a combination of political and legal rights typical of modern liberal democracies. There is some overlap with the *Bill of Rights, 1960*. While most are individual rights, some are collective in nature. Some rights reflect particular Canadian historical circumstances, such as sections 16 to 22 on languages and section 23 on education. Section 25 of the Charter refers to aboriginal rights recognized under the *Royal Proclamation of 1763* and land claims settlements and section 35 affirms aboriginal and treaty rights. The equality rights provision, section 15, attempts to protect initiatives designed for disadvantaged groups where there is conflict with individual rights. The Charter is not to be interpreted so as to deny already existing rights (*e.g.*, those provided by the *Canadian Bill of Rights* or federal and provincial human rights codes).

2. APPLICATION OF THE CHARTER

The Charter applies exclusively to the laws and actions of the state which allegedly conflict with the rights described above. The Charter does not apply to rights violations or discrimination by private interests or non-state organizations. For instance, if a citizen applied for a job in the private sector, but is denied that job because of racial background, there is no violation of Charter rights. However, there may be a violation of other human rights legislation. Human rights and the Charter will be examined in further detail in Chapter Eight.

Under section 24 of the Charter, individuals or groups are given "standing" to challenge laws or official actions by allowing anyone suffering infringement of Charter rights to apply to the courts for "such remedy as the court considers appropriate and just in the circumstances." The application for remedies and judicial review of alleged rights violations is not confined to legislation, although many important Charter decisions involve the striking down of laws as unconstitutional. In *Operation Dismantle v. The Queen*[13] a request was made for a court order

---
[13]   [1985] 1 S.C.R. 441.

prohibiting testing of American cruise missiles in Canada on the ground that they posed an increased risk of nuclear war and thereby violated the section 7 Charter rights to life, liberty and security of the person. Although the request failed because the Supreme Court of Canada was not satisfied that there was a causal link between the decision to test and the threat of nuclear war, the court did hold that courts can scrutinize cabinet decisions, and the exercise of all government prerogatives or executive decisions, for compliance with the Charter. Section 24 also allows for the exclusion from court proceedings of evidence obtained in a manner that infringed rights or freedoms. The impact of this provision on police and prosecutorial procedures has been one of largest areas of Charter controversy.

3. HOW THE CHARTER WORKS

The rights set out in the Charter are not absolute. Quite apart from conflicts between rights, and the fact that certain rights are restricted to certain persons (*e.g.*, the right to vote is limited to Canadian citizens), courts must take other competing interests into account. In reviewing laws and official actions, the courts are asked to weigh public interests that justify laws or official actions against rights said to be violated.

Section 1 of the Charter is the primary mechanism of this process of judicial review. First, the courts consider whether the law or official action in question does indeed violate a Charter right. Secondly, if a violation is found, the court then considers whether it can be sufficiently justified on public policy grounds. As the section itself states, all Charter rights are subject "to such reasonable limits prescribed by law as can be demonstrably justified in a free and democratic society." The court, then, is being asked whether there is an adequate balance between public interests and rights; if one is not found then the law or action in question may be held as unconstitutional.

In evaluating whether restrictions or limits on rights are both reasonable and demonstrably justifiable, Chief Justice Dickson set out criteria in *R. v. Oakes*[14] and *R. v. Edwards Books and Art*.[15] He held that two requirements must be satisfied. First, the legislative objective that the limitation is designed to promote must be of sufficient importance to warrant overriding a constitutional right. It must bear on a "pressing and substantial concern." Second, the means chosen to attain those objectives must be proportional or appropriate to the ends.

---

[14] [1986] 1 S.C.R. 103.
[15] [1986] 2 S.C.R. 713.

The proportionality requirement has three aspects: the limiting measures must be carefully designed and rationally connected to the objective; they must impair rights as little as possible; and their effects must not so severely interfere with rights that the legislative objective is outweighed by the abridgement of rights. The Supreme Court stated that the nature of the proportionality test would vary depending on the circumstances. The courts have been careful to avoid rigid and inflexible standards both in articulating the standard of proof and in describing the criteria comprising the proportionality requirement.

Section 52(1) of the *Constitution Act, 1982*, declares the constitution to be the supreme law of Canada and any law that is inconsistent with it (including the Charter) is of no force or effect. Some commentators claim that this provision establishes the supremacy of rights as set out in the Charter at the expense of parliamentary supremacy. However, this assertion is answered by reference to section 33, the much misunderstood and seldom-used "notwithstanding" clause, a provision that gives the final say to the elected legislatures in the event of diasagreement with the courts. It authorises Parliament or a legislature to override a decision of the court finding violation of the fundamental freedoms, legal and equality rights set out in sections 2 and 7 to 15 of the Charter. After a period of five years such laws expire or can again be challenged in the courts. The political costs of invoking section 33 are high but the principle of parliamentary supremacy is also preserved.

However, conflicts between the courts and legislatures are seldom deep enough to justify resort to the notwithstanding clause. With some exceptions, the courts have tended to defer to the will of the legislatures on the matter of public interest justifications. For the most part, where legislation has failed to meet section 1 requirements, the legislature in question has been given the opportunity to correct technical failings in the legislation. Sometimes laws have been struck down in their entirety and legislatures have chosen to drop them altogether.

Occasionally, the courts have ventured so far as to amend legislation on their own, in effect rewriting it through particular interpretation and application. In these situations judges have used the Charter to substitute their own views of public policy for the elected representatives' formulation of public policy in legislation. This rewriting has caused some to call for the more frequent use of section 33 and for greater scrutiny of judicial appointments and performance. Criminal justice officials have also argued that the Charter makes it more difficult to enforce the law effectively. Still, others argue that the Charter makes it easier to take political issues out of the hands of citizens and responsible elected politicians and put them into the hands of lawyers and appointed judges.

The Charter has certainly given the courts an opportunity to rule in a wider range of issues affecting Canadians. It has substantially increased judges' powers to reflect on the constitutionality of laws and official actions, and to authoritatively question legislation and public procedures. There is some danger of judges usurping what are properly political functions. However, many constitutional law specialists answer the critics by pointing out that the power to strike down legislation has been exercised carefully within the context of the circumstances of each case and established judicial principles. They argue that the Charter has created a new "dialogue" between the courts and the legislatures which has had the effect of improving our laws.

The *Canadian Charter of Rights and Freedoms* establishes a delicate and uniquely Canadian balance between legislative and judicial power. Part of the future of Canadian constitutional law lies in how this balance is worked out in yet further Charter challenges. Some are concerned about the widening political influence of judges while others argue that judges should have the final say in conflicts between rights and public policy. We will return to these debates in Chapter Eight.

While the Charter attempts to reflect values that all Canadians can identify with, the fact remains that there is much unresolved business in the Canadian constitution. Should the Senate be reformed? Do the provinces have too much or too little power? Will constitutional change be possible with our new amendment processes? Perhaps most importantly, the future of Canadian constitutional law also lies in attempts to accommodate the self-determination aspirations of groups, such as natives and francophones, that consider themselves nations within the Canadian state. The Supreme Court's secession ruling and the response of Parliament and the Quebec National Assembly are but the most recent developments on this front. These formidable constitutional challenges mean that Canada may yet face fundamental constitutional change in the future.

FURTHER READING

A.V. Dicey, *Introduction to the Study of the Constitution* (London: Macmillan, 1981)

P.W. Hogg, *Constitutional Law of Canada*, 4th ed. (Toronto: Carswell, 1998)

R. Knopff & F.L. Morton, *The Charter Revolution and the Court Party* (Calgary: Broadview Press, 2000)

J.R. Mallory, *The Structure of Canadian Government* (Toronto: Gage, 1984)

M. Mandel, *The Charter of Rights and the Legalization of Politics in Canada* rev'd. ed. (Toronto: Thompson, 1994)

M.H. Ogilvie, *Historical Introduction to Legal Studies* (Toronto: Carswell, 1982)

P.H. Russell, *Leading Constitutional Decisions*, 4th ed. (Ottawa: Carleton University Press, 1987)

P.H. Russell, *The Judiciary in Canada: The Third Branch of Government* (Toronto: McGraw-Hill, Ryerson, 1987)

R.J. Van Loon & M.S. Whitington, *The Canadian Political System*, 3rd ed. (Toronto: McGraw-Hill, Ryerson, 1981)

Chapter Four

The Different Areas of Law: Substantive Law Doctrines

Canada's laws are extensive, filling hundreds of volumes, and have entire law libraries devoted to them. With so many statutes, regulations and reported cases, some classification is necessary in order to adequately organize and comprehend them and to work out their applicability to real situations.

Laws are classified and differentiated in many ways. We can distinguish between federal and provincial laws, as we saw in Chapter Three. We can also distinguish between legislation and judge-made laws based on precedent, as we saw in Chapter Two.

As we also saw in Chapter Two, we can make distinctions between legal systems. These include common law and civil law systems, which have been imported into many nations, as well as indigenous or customary law systems. Further distinctions may be made between domestic national laws and international laws, which largely govern relations between states involving treaties, conventions, and the rules set by organizations such as the United Nations. Religious laws such as Canon, Rabbinical and Islamic laws do not belong to any particular state, or govern relations between states but nonetheless govern the conduct of their adherents.

For practical purposes, a distinction may also be made between substantive laws and procedural laws. This practical distinction tends to be the most important one within Canadian common law systems. Generally speaking, substantive law tells us what our rights and duties are, while procedural law tells us how to enforce them. So, criminal law lays down offences that prohibit certain activities while the law of criminal procedure regulates the enforcement, prosecution and trial of those who break the criminal law. Likewise, contract law regulates the rights and obligations of contracting parties, while the law of civil procedure regulates the

LEGAL SYSTEMS

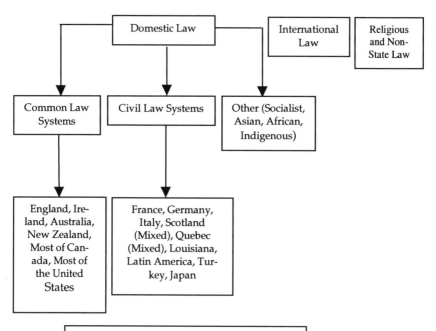

Note: Scots law is based on Roman law but much affected by common law. Federal laws applying in Quebec, notably criminal law, have common law origins.

methods of enforcing those rights by suing in court. Substantive law, then, is in a sense primary, while procedural law is supplementary, qualifying the substantive law in its application (procedural law is also sometimes referred to as adjectival law).

This substantive/procedural law distinction is somewhat arbitrary. The law of evidence, which comprises rules about what facts may be admitted in court, what sort of proof is required, and what sort of questions may be put to witnesses, is a closer fit with procedural than substantive law. In some respects, however, it deals with matters rather different from those concerning procedural law (*e.g.*, service of writs, drafting of pleadings, methods of appeal), so that it warrants a category of its own. Sometimes special procedures are included with particular substantive laws, such as those accompanying the *Controlled Drugs and Substances Act.*[1]

Procedural laws and evidence will be discussed in detail in Chapter Five. This chapter focuses on substantive law and its various categories or types of laws. Many people tend to distinguish between criminal law (dealing with punishment) and civil law (dealing with rights and compensation). While this distinction is highly relevant to procedure, as we shall see in Chapter Five, it is not sufficiently comprehensive for the purposes of classifying substantive law. The use of the term civil law also tends to cause confusion with civil law systems described in previous chapters. A more accurate conceptual distinction in the area of substantive law is between public law and private law.

The classification of law as public or private depends on whether it involves issues of public or private interest. Public law, as its name suggests, regulates the institutions of the state, their relations with one another and their relations with the citizen. It includes constitutional law and administrative regulations that govern the various activities of the state. It also includes criminal law, where the state prohibits activity in the public interest and deploys public institutions to enforce the law and punish offenders. On the other hand, private law is primarily concerned about individual interests or those organized interests that serve private purposes. Included are laws regulating matters of contract, tort, property and the family.

This distinction between public and private law is also somewhat arbitrary. Public law affects the private interests. Individual victims are directly affected by most criminal offences and they have an obvious interests in the operation of criminal law. Contracts and the activities of private corporations affect collective economic life. The regulation of the family has enormous impact on collective social life. Although the "public/private" distinction is not always clear in practice, and indeed is sometimes contested or disputed, we will nonetheless adopt this formal conceptual distinction in this brief survey of the primary areas of public and private law, applicable in Canadian common law jurisdictions.

The categories of substantive and procedural law, and public and private law may be summed up in the following way:

---

[1]   S.C. 1996, c. 19.

CATEGORIES OF SUBSTANTIVE AND PROCEDURAL LAW

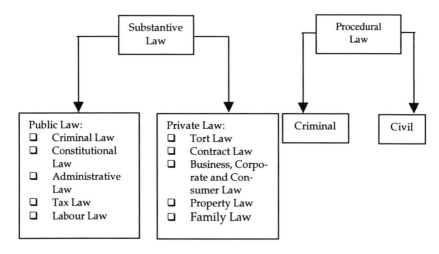

I. PUBLIC LAW

Constitutional law, surveyed in the previous chapter, is one of the major areas of public law. Criminal law is another. Adminstrative and taxation law will be surveyed later in this section.

A. Criminal Law

Of all areas of law perhaps the most visible is criminal law. This is the area of law that forms the subject of countless books, movies and television shows. This, too, is an area where there is intense policy debate and where the ordinary citizen, whether as witness, victim, accused or juror, has a good chance of coming into contact with the law.

Not only is the criminal law one of the most visible area of law, it is also arguably the most significant. For criminal law, more than any other area of law, lays down the ground rules of society and dictates what conduct is unacceptable. It prohibits activity defined by the state as harmful or anti-social. The prohibited activity is so grave that public interests are thought to be involved, as well as the obvious interests of victims. Criminal law also dictates what excuses, justifications and defences are allowed for otherwise prohibited activity. In these ways, criminal law expresses the dominant values in a society.

Until the eighteenth century, much of the criminal law was created and developed by the judges in the form of common law. As England underwent rapid industrialization and urbanization, criminal law increasingly took statutory form. Law reformers such as Jeremy Bentham argued that the next logical step was to comprehensively codify the criminal law.

There was also transformation in the administration of criminal law. Professional policing and public (or Crown) prosecutions displaced the role of the victim, some of the functions of the justice of the peace, and agents acting on behalf of both. Lawyers increasingly represented accused persons, counterbalancing, to some extent, the increased presence of the state in the enforcement of criminal law. The penitentiary increasingly displaced a system of capital punishment for most serious offences, which had in practice been mitigated by discretionary pardons, where condemned convicts faced lesser punishments such as transportation. These institutional reforms gave rise to a more rational and certain criminal justice system. They also created a system that more effectively confronted the increase in crime that resulted from the industrial revolution, simply because far greater numbers of offenders could be dealt with.

Bentham's call for codification of criminal law was never realized in England although it was in Canada. In 1867, criminal law was placed placed under the jurisdiction of the Dominion Parliament. It took the federal government a quarter century to consolidate the colonial criminal laws as received and developed in the provinces, and to organize them in a comprehensive codified form. In 1892, Parliament incorporated criminal law into a special statute, the Canadian *Criminal Code*.

The current Canadian *Criminal Code*[2] spells out most crimes, setting out offences and the maximum penalty attached. It also sets out defences. Elements of our criminal law still remain outside the Code, however. The legal principles of liability, the mental and physical elements of the offence that must be proved, are largely governed by common law principles. Common law defences, (*e.g.*, intoxication), are still available. Some offences, like drug offences, are to be found in other statutes, (*e.g.*, the *Food and Drugs Act*[3] or the *Controlled Drugs and Substances Act*). And there are many provincial offences, which, though not strictly crimes, are prosecuted like crimes. In fact, close to 70 per cent of prosecutions are for road traffic offences.

The reason for distinguishing between crimes (created by federal legislation) and provincial offences, or quasi-crimes (created by provincial legislation), has to do with the divisions of law-making powers in the

---

[2]   R.S.C. 1985, c. C-46.
[3]   R.S.C. 1985, c. F-27.

Constitution Act, 1867.[4] Federal Parliament has been given the jurisdiction to make criminal law. However, provinces are allowed to make laws imposing penalties for violations of their own provincial laws and this is the source of their authority to create provincial offences.

Under the *Constitution Act, 1867,* the provinces also have jurisdition over the administration of justice in a province, including criminal law. Most policing takes place under provincial authority (the RCMP are "contracted out" to provinces and municipal policing takes place under authority delegated from the provincial governments). Most prosecutions are brought by Crown prosecutors who are appointed by the provinces.

Distinguishing between a "special part" and a "general part" is helpful in understanding these aspects of Canadian criminal law. The first provides definitions of offences and specifies penalties for them. The latter are the rules relating to jurisdiction, liability and defences.

The special part of Canadian criminal law consists of about 300 *Criminal Code* sections and numerous other sections in federal statutes and regulations, defining countless criminal offences. We may usefully group these into eight categories:

1. Offences of violence against the person including murder, manslaughter and non-fatal assaults;
2. Sex offences (*e.g.*, sexual assault);
3. Offences of dishonesty against property (*e.g.*, theft, fraud);
4. Offences causing damage to property (*e.g.*, arson and malicious mischief);
5. Offences against the state (*e.g.*, treason, sedition);
6. Offences against order (*e.g.*, riot, unlawful assembly);
7. Offences threatening social institutions (*e.g.*, forgery, perjury, interfering with justice); and
8. Miscellaneous "nuisance" offences against morality and welfare (*e.g.*, obscenity, gambling and public nuisance).

The general part of criminal law is to be found partly in the *Criminal Code* and partly in common law and is largely concerned with principles of liability and with general defences. The basic principle of criminal liability is summed up in the Latin maxim, *actus non facit reum, nisi mens sit rea.* This means literally that an act does not make you guilty unless your mind is guilty too. Did the accused physically commit the offence and know that he or she was doing so? Accordingly, liability for

---

[4]   (U.K.), 30 & 31 Vict., c. 3, reprinted in R.S.C. 1985, App. II, No. 5.

an offence has two components, what is termed the *actus reus* (the physical aspect of committing an offence) and the *mens rea* (the mental element, which may consist of an attitude of intention, recklessness or awareness of committing an offence). The *actus reus* of murder, for example, is causing the victim's death, the *mens rea* is usually an intention to kill or an awareness that one's act is likely to kill. We will examine the required standards of proof in criminal proceedings (the presumption of innocence and how the Crown must prove its case beyond a reasonable doubt) in Chapter Five.

General defences consist of exemptions, excuses or justifications. Exemptions, which include infancy and insanity, take a defendant outside the ordinary operation of the criminal law. Such persons are deemed not sufficiently aware to be held responsible for their offences. Excuses, which include duress, necessity and mistake of fact, serve to negate culpability for a wrongful act. Handing the bank's money over to a bank robber is wrong, but one has no criminal liability for doing so at gunpoint. Justifications, which include the prevention of crime, execution of legal process and effecting lawful arrest, turn an otherwise wrongful act into a right and lawful one. To lay hands on people is normally considered assault, but not if you are lawfully arresting them.

Finally, a word on the aims and purposes of the criminal law. Most people agree that criminal law, which can involve drastic interference with people's liberty, cannot be justified unless it furthers some useful social purpose. This is the justification for the state's extensive presence in the form of police, Crown prosecutions and in the resources committed to the infliction of punishment. It is argued that one of the purposes served is the protection of individuals and society from the further occurrence of crimes. Another is to vindicate justice by punishing bad behaviour and to articulate shared values which are seen to be essential to social order. Whether such social aims or public interests are actually served by criminal law, and with what success, is a matter of continuing controversy.

Some argue that criminal law and its adminstration serves the interests of the powerful, while others point out misplaced priorities on matters such as drugs and prostitution, or misguided lenience towards certain groups such as young offenders. Still others are concerned about the balance struck between public and individual interests. Many point out, drawing from historical experience, that the rights of the accused relate ultimately to civil liberties, and in this respect they are a constitutional check on the some of the most interventionist and repressive measures available to the state. At the same time, however, many also argue that the rights of victims are neglected. Conservative critics tend to stress that the rights of the accused are advanced at the expense of the interests of victims and social protection. Others argue that the bureaucratic priorities of state institutions result in neglect of the victim. There is a great deal of debate around all these questions, and other complex and contentious issues involving criminal law and its administration.

B. Administrative Law

Like constitutional law, administrative law deals with the relations between the institutions of the state and the individual. The difference between them is one of level and detail. As we saw in the previous chapter, constitutional law provides the ground rules for the government of a society. Administrative law provides the detailed regulations for its day-to-day operation. Constitutional law gives the basic framework, administrative law the detailed superstructure. Administrative law conflicts tend to involve the more routine disputes involving the state.

To appreciate the operation of administrative law we can take a simple model of the working of our government. Basically, it operates as a series of mandates and responses. The electorate gives a mandate to our legislators. Through legislation and the creation of agencies and tribunals, the legislators give more specific mandates and powers to the executive branch of government. Government administrators implement legislation, exercise the powers conferred on them by legislation, and issue detailed regulations under the authority of legislation. In this manner, public policy is administered in areas where government intervention is deemed important.

As government is called upon to meet more and more of our needs, the statutory powers conferred upon administrators grow increasingly numerous and complex. The determination of the practical powers given to an administrator by the relevant statute, the correction of administative mistakes, and the provision of redress or compensation for those mistakes are the matters that concern the courts in administrative law disputes. With the growth of the state since the nineteenth century, the courts have been increasingly asked to strike a balance between government intervention and effectiveness and individual fairness and rights.

An important part of administrative law involves the analysis and review of adminstrative powers conferred by legislation. Did the agency or official have the authority to act as they did? Did they respect the rights of persons affected by their actions? Were the regulations within their powers to pass?

Basically, there are two kinds of control provided by administrative law. There are institutional controls within the government itself, (*e.g.*, tribunals and appeal boards). Outside the government there are judicial controls, subject to most of the advantages and disadvantages associated with law courts: independence, delay and costliness.

There are two kinds of judicial control of administrative action. First, there is the right to appeal to a judge granted by statute; and second, a similar right to judicial review under the common law. The former right exists only if it is expressly provided for in legislation and involves a reconsideration by a court of an administrative decision. The latter allows the court to review all administrative actions and decisions. Under this common law review, the court determines whether an administrative body or official had jurisdiction to act as it did and whether the actions were carried out in accordance with the principles of natural justice.

Judicial review on the basis of jurisdiction involves a determination of whether the administrative action or decision was authorized by the relevant statute or was *ultra vires* (beyond the administrator's powers). This form of review is available to control almost all administrative decisions affecting the public. It exists by virtue of the common law, except where it has been streamlined and augmented by legislation, and is available unless specifically excluded by statute. The most straightforward kind of judicial review occurs where administrators violate an express condition in the statute on which their power depends.

Even without violation of an express statutory provision, there may be still be grounds for judicial review. The courts can also review whether an official or administrative tribunal acted or decided in such a way as to violate common law principles of natural justice. These essentially involve a review of the fairness of administrative proceedings. The most common of such violations is failure to give people affected by administrative decisions adequate notice or a prior opportunity to be heard on their own behalf.

If an administrative action or decision is invalid on the basis of jurisdiction or natural justice, the courts may order various remedies. Further adminstrative action may be prohibited (*prohibition*). Or, the court can in effect substitute its own decision by ordering that a decision be made again taking into account considerations raised by the court (*certiorari*). Courts can also order administrators to perform an action that has not been performed where a duty is found to do so (*mandamus*).

Administrators may also be liable for any harm resulting from their actions. If found to have acted without statutory authority and if their action constituted a tort (see below), administrators may be made to compensate persons injured by their action. Government administrators, unless specially protected by statute or a crown immunity, are subject to the same rules as the rest of society.

In Canada, as in most common law jurisdictions, administrative law is part of ordinary law and disputes are taken to the regular courts of law. The Federal Court of Canada serves as the destination for the trial and appeal of federal adminstrative law disputes, although its decisions may also be appealed to the Supreme Court of Canada, like those of courts dealing with provincial adminstrative disputes. This is in contrast to the *droit administratif* and separate hierarchy of specialized administrative law courts found in France.

Supporters of judicial review point out that the courts play an important part in upholding individual rights against a state that is too readily or bluntly interventionist. However, there are also critics of judicial review. They argue that judges too often interfere with public policy matters in areas where they have little expertise. Historically, the courts have tended to express conservative hostility to public state interventions. Critics suggest that specialized administrative courts, like those in France, would overcome these problems.

C. Tax Law

In many respects, the disputes that concern tax law are adminstative law disputes. However, tax law is a distinct and large area of substantive doctrine that many lawyers consider a specialized field of law. In this respect tax law is similar to labour law. In addition to employment standards and worker compensation issues, labour law includes elaborate legal rules and regulations governing the recognition of unions, collective bargaining, the exercise of the right to strike, and the appeal of grievances to labour arbitration boards. Judicial review through adminstrative law principles does take place in this large area of specialized and substantive law, just as it can in the tax law field.

Simply stated, a tax is a compulsory contribution levied on individuals, firms or property, intended to transfer resources from the private to the public sector. Tax law permeates society and is an area of law that touches every citizen at some point. For example, the purchase of an automobile involves the payment of a number of taxes federal sales tax and perhaps tariffs, which are included in the purchase price, and provincial sales tax, which is paid on that purchase price. To drive the automobile, the driver must have a driver's licence (for which a fee is paid) and pay annual fees to register the car and obtain licence plates, all of which are forms of tax. Taxes are also paid on the gas, oil and parts to keep the car running. And, on top of all these taxes, it must be remembered that federal and provincial income taxes have been paid on the money earned to make these purchases.

One may ask, "Why do we have all these taxes and how do they become a matter of concern to the law?" The simple answer is that governments require revenues in order to finance certain public expenditures such as defence, law and order, public parks, education and health services, to name but a few. In earlier times taxes were often levied at the whim of the ruler. Over the centuries, though, the citizens in most civilized countries forced the rulers not to tax without the authority of the elected representatives of the people. Thus, today, taxes can only be imposed by legislation set out in the various taxing statutes, regulations and bylaws.

In Canada, the power to impose taxes is divided between the federal Parliament and the provincial legislatures. The division of taxing powers is set out in the *Constitution Act, 1867*, which provides in section 91(3) that the federal Parliament can raise money by "any mode or system of taxation" and provides in section 92(2) that the provinces are limited to "direct taxation within the province." A direct tax is demanded from the very person who is expected to pay it, for example, provincial sales tax that is paid by the customer when purchasing the goods. Indirect tax is demanded from one person with the expectation and intention that it will be passed on to someone else, for example, excise tax on alcohol which is paid by the manufacturer and passed on to the consumer by being included in the sale price.

As can be seen, the federal taxing powers are much wider than the provincial taxing powers. Because of the economic power that goes with taxation, the issue of the redistribution of taxing powers between the federal government and the provinces has been one of the stumbling blocks in constitutional change for Canada.

There is also a third level of taxation imposed, that is, at the municipal level. Municipalities and similar bodies are able to impose taxes on the basis of taxing powers delegated to them by the provinces. A city can impose realty taxes on the owners of property within the city or business taxes on businesses carried on within the city.

Taxes can only be imposed by legislation and the legislation must be within the competence of the enacting body. Thus citizens may dispute liability for taxes on the grounds that either the taxing body lacked the authority to pass the law or that the taxing statute does not bring them within its net. In this way, the tax laws may be brought before the courts to be questioned and interpreted and, in consequence, a large body of case law has grown up relating to taxation in addition to the legislation itself.

II. PRIVATE LAW

We now turn to private law, so called because it involves the regulation of disputes between individuals or private groups. Private law largely deals with individuals' rights and duties *vis-à-vis* each other, as opposed to public law, which largely concerns their rights and duties *vis-à-vis* the state. Such rights and duties arise from various sources; from civil wrongs called torts, from contractual agreements, from ownership of property, and from family relationships.

The responsibility of enforcing rights and duties in these areas lie in the hands of an individual or private party. The state merely provides the legal rules and the forum of courts for these disputes to be heard. As we will see in the next chapter, private law proceedings are sometimes called civil proceedings, involving different procedures and standards of proof than criminal proceedings. The aggrieved party seeking compensation for some harm or loss is called a plaintiff.

Most private laws fall under provincial jurisdiction, under the "property and civil rights" provision of section 92 of the *Constitution Act, 1867*. Private law, in consequence, varies across Canada. In Quebec, for example, it consists of civil law rules, while in the rest of Canada such matters are regulated by the common law. And even in the rest of Canada the common law rules on contract, tort and property may vary from province to province. We cannot, therefore, properly talk of the Canadian law of contract, for example; we have to talk of the contract law of Alberta, Manitoba, Saskatchewan and so on.

All the same, within the provinces other than Quebec, the differing common law rules are all based on the same fundamental principles. These can best be seen at work in the three central areas of common law; contract, tort and property. This chapter looks briefly at these three historically important branches of law, together with one further subject, which is of immense contemporary social significance, family law. Consumer laws and corporate, business and commercial laws, which supplement the contract law area, play an important role in modern economic life, but lie beyond the scope of a concise introductory survey.

A. Tort Law

Tort law plays a prominent role in the history of the common law. Tort is simply French for "wrong". A tort is a private or civil wrong, as contrasted with a public or criminal wrong.

The common law distinction between crimes and civil wrongs is tied up with the Norman Conquest and the establishment of centrally administered courts, as discussed in Chapter Two. When wrongdoing was seen to simply affect the victim and the peace of the local community there was no meaningful distinction between crime and tort. The introduction of the notion of the King's Peace made possible the distinction between wrongdoing involving broader public interests and those affecting the individual alone. Matters deemed too important to be left to the victim alone for redress were handled by the new royal courts of justice, presided over by locally appointed magistrates and judges on assize circuits. This justified an extensive administrative presence through England, which some argue was more significant to the security of the state than a large standing army. Victims of crime could not obtain compensation from the criminal courts. They, along with those who who suffered wrongdoings not considered crime, had recourse to the civil courts.

Torts are distinguished by several features. As suggested above and elaborated in the next chapter, torts involve civil proceedings that are rather different than criminal proceedings. Civil wrongs are usually set right in terms of compensation, while crimes are redressed by punishment. Civil wrongs are not wrongs if the victim consents to them, while some crimes remain crimes despite the victim's consent; one cannot be absolved of murder by the fact that the victim consented. However, a tort, unlike civil wrongs arising out of breach of contract, need not arise out of an agreement or special relationship. A tort, as the term implies, is a mere wrong that incurs legal liability where legal obligations of a general sort are owed.

When does an act constitute a tort? Ideally, it would be convenient to simply say that any act or omission is a tort if it harms another. However, this is not true. Many acts may be harmful without necessarily constituting torts. It is no tort to refrain, as a bystander, from rescuing a drowning swimmer you could easily save. Whether an act is a tort depends on what the courts and legislatures have historically recognized as obligations that create liability for a tort.

The sort of torts recognized by law are too numerous to classify easily. They include: trespass to the person (*i.e.*, assault and battery); trespass to land and trespass to goods; negligence (*i.e.*, failing to take reasonable care and thereby injuring another); nuisance (*i.e.*, creating a situation that is dangerous or offensive to your neighbour or to the public); libel and slander (*i.e.*, written or spoken defamation of character); and deceit or fraud. Up until the late nineteenth century, intentional torts predominated because the courts tended to favour the principle of no liability without clear fault.

In the modern day, torts caused by negligence have become more important than intentional torts. Modern life and consumer culture makes us increasingly dependent on the actions of others and subject to accidents, injury or illness caused by defective products. The state has intervened to regulate more economic and social areas. In many cases, duties are set out in consumer protection legislation, and in health and safety standards in various areas and institutional settings such as public roads and highways and the workplace. Where legislation fails to set out a standard, the common law applies. The English House of Lords decision *Donoghue v. Stevenson*[5] set out the common law formulation of negligence in clearest terms. The plaintiff must establish that the defendant had a duty of care, defined in terms of a responsibility to avoid actions that can be reasonably foreseen to cause harm to others.

Like criminal law, the law of tort has defences. These include "act of God" (I cannot be held liable for a tree-fall on my land damaging your home if the tree-fall was caused by lightning); the plaintiff's own assumption of risk (a visitor who jumps into the lion's cage cannot sue the zoo for being mauled); and the plaintiff's own wrongdoing (burglars breaking into my house cannot complain if the stairs are so unsafe that they fall down them and are injured).

Remedies for tort fall into two categories. The main remedy is compensation; this is the reason most victims of road accidents, for instance, go to court. Damages are often difficult to calculate, especially those relating to economic loss. In some circumstances, damages may not be enough. For instance, if neighbours make so much noise each night that I can never get to sleep, I shall be less interested in damages than in getting them to stop making noise. Here I shall sue for an injunction, which is an order to the wrongdoer (or tortfeasor) to desist.

What is the social purpose of the law of tort? As we have seen, tort law serves a number of functions. In some cases (*e.g.*, the case of the noisy neighbour) tort law may serve to stop the wrongdoing. In others (*e.g.*, in cases of libel) it may serve to put things right by vindicating the plaintiff's reputation. In most cases (*e.g.*, motor accidents), it operates to award compensation. Obtaining compensation, however, depends on a

---

[5]   [1932] A.C. 562.

variety of factors (can you find the wrongdoer, can you prove your case against the wrongdoer, can the latter pay?) so tort law has been called a "forensic lottery".

In many common law jurisdictions, tort claims around workplace health and safety have been removed from the civil courts and are dealt with by specialized tribunals such as the Workers Compensation Board. In several provinces, torts in the context of road accidents have been replaced by a system of "no fault" insurance, so that the victim gets compensation without having to sue for it. In the 1960s, New Zealand experimented with replacing all forms of tort claims with a state administered compensation scheme.

Studies show that insurance companies often play an dominant role when tort claims are left for resolution in the civil courts. In fact, very few of these legal claims are resolved by the courts, most are settled by informal negotiation before or after litigation commences. This negotiation between a potential plaintiff and an insurance company representing the tortfeasor is mostly unregulated. Some point out that such negotiations are seldom between equals, and as a result, they are oriented more to the insurance company's "bottom line" than a fair settlement for the claimant.

On the other hand, many personal injury lawyers and insurance companies are opposed to state accident compensation schemes, preferring free market to government solutions. Quite apart from the self-interests of these groups, the experience has been that leaving compensation in the hands of the state often results in costly and inefficient bureaucracies that lack sufficient funds to provide satisfactory compensation. Moreover, if one of social aims of torts is to deter risky and negligent behaviour, state compensation schemes tend to ignore the allocation of fault, whereas this is a primary aim of the courts. How to best strike a satisfactory balance between compensation and liability is one of the ongoing debates in this field of law.

B. Contract Law

Contract is said to form the basis of the laws of commerce. It certainly plays a prominent part in the history of the common law, particularly in the eighteenth and nineteenth centuries. Free enterprise or laissez-faire policies, and the view that the government should interfere as little as possible with commerce, became dominant in England in the eighteenth and nineteenth centuries and facilitated the British Empire's domination of world trade. It was thought that a free market economy should leave individuals as free as possible to make whatever contracts they choose.

It followed from these policies that economic (and even social and political) rights and obligations should be based as far as possible on express or implied agreements between freely contracting parties. The common law doctrines that developed around contract reflected these ideas and were intended to contribute to economic stability and growth by creating certainty and predictability in economic transactions.

What, then, is a contract? Basically, it is a formal agreement between two or more parties with legally binding rights and obligations. A contract does not have to be written or follow a standard form. In order to be recognized as a contract it does, however, require four elements: an offer, acceptance of an offer, an intention to create legal relations, and consideration or some benefit of value to the contracting parties.

To begin with the third and fourth elements: There must exist between the parties an intention to create legal relations. If you and I agreed to go for a walk by the canal, there would be no contract because neither of us would intend to bring about any legal relationship in such a case. There must also be a *quid pro quo* on each side of the agreement. Each must give, do or promise something by way of consideration for the other's promise. A bare promise by me to give you my hat, unsupported by your promise to give me something in return (called "consideration" in the law), is not legally binding. The common law of contract clearly requires a bargain, evidenced either by an actual exchange (often property or money), or by the clear exchange of promises.

How, are contracts formed? There are two stages: offer and acceptance, the first two elements of a legal contract identified above. In a typical contract of sale one party, the offerer, makes an offer to the other (*e.g.*, I offer to sell you my car for $5,000) and then the other party, the offeree, accepts the offer (*e.g.*, you tell me you agree to buy my car for $5,000). Alternatively, the buyer could have initiated proceedings by offering to buy and the seller could have accepted by agreeing to sell at the price offered. But until the offer is accepted, there is no contract.

So, in a contract of sale, which party makes the offer? After all, sales clerks and shoppers are not usually so formal as to say, "I offer," and "I accept." According to common law, when a shop offers goods for sale it does not actually make an offer; it makes what lawyers call an invitation to treat, inviting prospective buyers to engage in negotiation. Then, by picking up the goods and offering the money, the buyer makes the offer. As yet there is no contract until the sales clerk takes the money and thereby accepts the offer for the store-keeper.

What happens if there is a difference between offer and acceptance? Suppose I offer you something for $5 and you say, "I'll buy it for $4."

Here, the common law holds that there is no acceptance. Instead, there is a counter-offer, which "kills" my original offer and no contract arises unless and until I now accept your counter-offer. Even where the parties do agree and the offer and acceptance coincide, there still may be no contract. The agreement may be "vitiated" by some defect. For example, it may be void for illegality of purpose: contract with an assassin on someone's life is obviously not a valid legal contract. It may be void because of some mistake on the part of the parties, due to fraud or misrepresentation. Contracts are not binding on young children. Sometimes valid contracts can be unenforceable because they are not recorded in writing. Contracts for sale of land, for instance, will not be enforced unless in writing.

In practice, most legal problems around contracts do not have to do with the coinciding of offer and acceptance, or vitiating factors, but arise out of one of the parties breaking the contract by defaulting on his or her obligations. This is the point at which the other party starts looking for legal remedies for breach of contract. What are a contracting party's remedies for breach of contract? The most common is to sue for damages by way of compensation. The offending party may have to put you back financially in the position you would have been in had the contract not been broken. In certain cases, however, especially in contracts for sale of land and houses, damages may not suffice, and the wronged party will sue for specific performance. The court may order the offending party to carry out the contract, most contract disputes involve determination of appropriate remedies.

It is important to understand this area of legal doctrine in its modern economic context. Doing so raises questions about the centrality of contract and the economic assumptions upon which contract law has developed.

Studies show that, in practice, many modern businesses will avoid contracts, especially if they have ongoing relations with another party. Flexibility is preferred, with differences ironed out through continual negotiation. If relations break down businesses will attempt to negotiate a compromise, sometimes with the assistance of a third party arbitrator, rather than resort to the courts searching for a contract, breach and remedies.

Many consumer contracts seldom reflect agreements freely entered into by parties with equal bargaining power. More often, businesses impose terms which few consumers fully comprehend but readily accept in order to gain access to a product. The injustices of the common law principle of *caveat emptor* (let the buyer beware) has been modified to some extent by courts reading in "implied terms". However, consumer protection and sale of goods legislation, government agencies and non-governmental consumer protection groups all have played the most important role in moderating the effects of classic common law contract principles.

C. Property Law

While contract law was at the centre of the economic and commercial activities of the industrial revolution, property law was at the centre of economic activities in the preceding hundreds of years back to the Norman Conquest. Historians point out that issues around land drove many of the medieval and early modern developments of the common law. Land was the chief item of wealth. Money, goods and chattels (the term originally meant "cattle") were comparatively less important, and stocks, shares and trust funds non-existent.

Common law divides property into realty and personalty. Realty denotes land and houses, things which in early Norman times a dispossessed owner could recover by a "real" action (an action to recover the thing itself). Personalty denotes money, goods and intangible property, things which could not be recovered in kind by a dispossessed owner. The dispossessed owner's only remedy, therefore, was a personal action for damages against the dispossessor.

Leases stand half-way between realty and personalty. Like realty (freehold estates) leases are interests in land. Like goods and chattels, leases could not be recovered in "real" actions. Curiously, then, leases formed part of a person's personalty and were termed "chattels real." Today, however, the law relating to leases and landlord-tenant relations is dealt with in textbooks along with the rest of land law.

Property law, then, falls into land law and personal property law. The latter involves rules concerning all the various transactions relating to goods: sale, hire, pledge, gift and bailment (*i.e.*, entrusting goods to another). Land law consists of rules relating to land transactions: sale, mortgage and lease.

Land transfer is naturally more complex than transfer of goods. For one thing, the transferor of goods can simply hand them over, but the transferor of land at common law had to convey by deed (a document which is signed, sealed and delivered). With goods the transferor's ownership is usually clear from having physical possession, whereas with land the conveyor's claim to ownership will only be accepted if the land was conveyed by someone, to whom it was conveyed by someone, to whom, *etc.*, until a "good root of title" is established. How far back you have to go depends on the jurisdiction: in Ontario 40 years is enough.

In Canada, as in many other common law countries, interests in land are registered. Actually, there are two systems in Canada: the registry office system and the newer land titles (or Torrens) system, which is also used in Australia and New Zealand. Under the former system, interests in land are recorded in a series of books in the registry office. Under the land titles system each parcel of land is recorded as a unit, all interests in it are recorded together in the land titles office, and the vendor's ownership is evidenced by a certificate of title issued by the office. Under both systems, however, the purchaser, or more likely the purchaser's lawyer, still has to search back through the registry books for records of the deeds of conveyance to determine whether there is a good root of title going back 40 or more years.

Other areas of property law include mortgages and other interests in land, which are also registered. There is also the complex area of trusts. The concept of the trust arose out of the old practice of conveying land to one person "to the use of" another. Since beneficiaries of such trusts were left unprotected by common law and needed assistance from equity, this whole area fell under the jurisdiction of equity. Today, a trust is a device serving to separate management from ownership: the manager is the trustee, the person with the legal estate, while the owner is the beneficiary with the equitable interest. Wills are yet another area of property law. Over the centuries common law developed a set of rules concerning wills and inheritance. It also created special rules concerning intestates (*i.e.*, people who die without making wills).

Although most of the basic common law principles around property are hundreds of years old, it should be noted that the boundaries of property law are not fixed. In Norman times the only things that could be owned were land, buildings, chattels and money. Later, negotiable instruments (*e.g.*, cheques), stocks and shares came into existence, which also formed the subject matter of ownership. More recently copyrights, trademarks and patents have been added to the list of items that can be owned. Intellectual property is one of the fastest growing areas of law today. Law-makers argue for legal recognition of property in yet other forms, such as economic privileges and job security. Who knows what tomorrow's generation may want to own?

D. Family Law

Family law deals primarily with three things: the founding of a family by marriage, the ending of a marriage by divorce, and the rights and duties of members of a family with respect to one another both during the marriage and after it has irretrievably broken down.

Although the *Constitution Act, 1867*, entrusts marriage and divorce to Parliament, federal governments avoided law-making in this particular area and instead, they allowed the provinces to rely on their jurisdiction over the "solemnization of marriage in the province." The rules as to age, formality and restrictions on marriage are to be found in the marriage legislation of the different provinces. Other areas of provincial jurisdiction were exercised to develop many of the other rules of family law in Canada. Family rights and duties during marriage and after marital breakdown arise partly from common law and partly from provincial statutes (*e.g.*, in Ontario, the *Child and Family Services Act*,[6] among others).

The federal government nonetheless has important specific areas of influence over family law. Parental rights to use force in lawful correction of their children, also a common law right, was written in to the *Criminal Code*, although today many are pressing for its abolition. The federal government's jurisdiction over divorce was exercised relatively recently. At common law a valid marriage could not be dissolved at all although divorces could be obtained by a private Act of Parliament. As a result, divorces were very rare and prosecutions for the offence of bigamy fairly frequent. Most breakdowns in marriage were handled by informal arrangements although courts also played an important role in giving formal recognition to separations.

Today, divorce is regulated by the *Divorce Act, 1985.*[7] The sole ground for divorce is marriage breakdown. Marriage breakdown can be established by showing that: (1) the parties have lived separate and apart for a year; (2) the spouse being divorced has been guilty of adultery since the marriage; or (3) one spouse has subjected the other to physical or mental cruelty.

The position of wives, who, at common law, were regarded to a large extent as one person with their husbands, and who, along with children, were treated virtually as if they were the property of the the male head of the family, was transformed both in England and in provinces by legislation from the mid-nineteenth century onwards. These statutes

---

[6]   R.S.O. 1990, c. C.11.
[7]   R.S.C. 1985, c. 3 (2nd Supp.).

had important implications in terms of property and parental rights and duties. They also transformed the common law concerning support and custody matters when marriages failed.

The increasing statutory interventions into family affairs from the mid-nineteenth century onwards reflected the realization that the state's involvement was necessary to confront the injustices facing women and children. Family laws were also seen as social policy tools to confront growing social problems, especially in urban areas. Public interests were therefore recognized in matters of family property, support and custody, which had been recognized largely as within the private sphere and under the prerogative of the male head of the family under the common law. More recently, specialized family courts and forms of alternative dispute resolution have developed as we will see in Chapter Six.

The family continues to pose enormous public policy challenges which are met, in large part, by family law. There is much debate currently over what constitutes a family. Traditionally only the nuclear family (*i.e.*, married opposite-sex couples with children) has garnered the attention of Canadian law-makers. However, over time, legislators increasingly afforded limited legal recognition to "common-law" relationships (permanent or semi-permanent unions between members of the opposite sex without formal marriages). In 1995, the Supreme Court of Canada largely extended the rights and duties of married couples to those involved in common law relationships.

The issue of same-sex relationships has proved much more contentious. Although the Government of Quebec recently introduced legislation that would make it the first jurisdiction in Canada to recognize same-sex relationships as akin to marriages for the purposes of provincial law-making, the National Assembly has not yet put the Bill to a final vote. Several years ago a similar law was defeated by legislators in Ontario when members of the governing party broke ranks and voted with opposition members against the Bill.

Although the Supreme Court of Canada has ruled unanimously that discrimination on the basis of sexual orientation is a violation of section 15(1) of the Charter it had, until recently, been sharply divided over the issue of whether to legally recognize same-sex relationships. In the past six years the court has taken up this issue on three separate occasions. It twice voted, first by a 4 to 3 margin, and later by a 5 to 4 margin, against the legal recognition of these relationships. However, in May of 1999, the court released its decision in the matter of *M. v. H.*[8] Eight of nine justices

---

[8]   [1999] 2 S.C.R. 3.

found the Ontario *Family Law Act*[9] to be unconstitutional because it does not give same-sex partners the right to seek spousal support from their former partners after the breakdown of their relationships.

This decision of the Supreme Court of Canada implies that same-sex relationships are to be given the same legal status as opposite-sex common law relationships. These broad implications were reflected only days after the decision when the Government of Canada passed legislation extending certain pension benefits to federal civil servants involved in same-sex relationships.

As we have seen, the political, social and economic contexts form an important dimension to the study of the various areas of substantive law doctrine. Politics and public policy cannot be divorced from the study of constitutional law examined in the previous chapter or of administrative and taxation law introduced in this chapter. Criminal law and family law are closely tied up with the ordering of social relations. Contract, tort and property law are central to the regulation of economic relations. And these laws, which are so closely connected to social and economic life, are also connected ultimately to public policies and politics. Consequently, they are, like the constitution, matters of contentious debate. The substantive law doctrines surveyed here are all important means of public intervention and of the management of the world around us so it is only natural that such debate takes place.

Lawyers, and students studying to be lawyers, are less concerned about these contexts of law and the public policy implications than the technical aspects of the doctrines introduced here. The identification of the relevant legal rules — some of the most basic ones have been outlined here — is their preoccupation. The practical identification and application of these rules in specific disputes involve the processes of legal reasoning discussed in chapter two. We further examine the institutional application of legal rules in the next chapter.

For those with broader and scholarly interests in the law, the study of its contexts, making sense of the patterns and purposes of the legal regulation of political, social and economic life, and the debates that arise, are all important issues. One way of making sense of these broader issues is to return to the theories introduced in Chapter One. We will return to some of these issues in the final chapter.

---

[9] R.S.O. 1990, c. F.3.

FURTHER READING

For a more detailed introductory and contextualized look at the areas of criminal, administrative, tort, contract and property law see Phil Harris, *An Introduction to Law*, 2nd ed. (London: Weidenfeld and Nicolson, 1984) Chapters 4, 5, 8, 9, 10 and 11. The following are more specialized texts on the substantive areas of law reviewed here (for Canadian constitutional law see Chapter Three):

Administrative Law:

S. Blake, *Administrative Law in Canada*, 2nd ed. (Toronto: Butterworths, 1997)

H.W.R. Wade, *Administrative Law*, 5th ed. (Oxford: Oxford University Press, 1982)

Contract Law, Consumers and Business:

G. Borrie & A.L. Diamond, *The Consumer, Society and the Law*, 4th ed. (Toronto: Penguin, 1981)

M.P. Furmston, *Chesire, Fifoot and Furmston's Law of Contract*, 13th ed. (London: Butterworths, 1996)

K.P. McGuinness, *The Law and Practice of Canadian Business Corporations* (Toronto: Butterworths, 1999)

J.E. Smyth, D.A. Soberman & A.J. Easson, *The Law and Business Administration in Canada*, 5th ed. (Toronto: Prentice Hall Canada Ltd., 1987)

Criminal Law:

Law Reform Commission of Canada, *Our Criminal Law* (1977) and *Recodifying Criminal Law* (Report No. 31, 1987).

A.W. Mewett & M. Manning, *Mewett and Manning on Criminal Law*, 3rd ed. (Toronto: Butterworths, 1994)

J.C. Smith & B. Hogan, *Criminal Law*, 6th ed. (London: Butterworths, 1988)

D. Stuart, *Canadian Criminal Law: A Treatise*, 2nd ed. (Toronto: Carswell, 1987)

Family Law:

P. Bromley, *Family Law* (London: Butterworths, 1992)

J. Eekelaar, *Family Law and Social Policy*, 2nd ed. (London: Weidenfeld and Nicolson, 1984)

D. Mendes da Costa, *Studies in Canadian Family Law* (Toronto: Butter-worths, 1982)

Property Law:

R.E. Megarry & H.W.R. Wade, *Law of Real Property* (London: Stevens, 1984)

McCallum, Sinclair, A.M., *Introduction to Real Property Law*, 4th ed. (Toronto: Butterworths, 1997)

Tort Law:

P.S. Atiyah, *Accidents, Compensation and the Law*, 3rd ed. (London: Weidenfeld and Nicolson, 1980)

A.M. Linden, *Canadian Tort Law*, 6th ed. (Toronto: Butterworths, 1997)

Chapter Five

The Law at Work:
Evidence and Procedure

As explained in the previous chapter, substantive law lays down our rights and duties, while procedural law provides for their enforcement and protection. Procedural law regulates the application of laws in the courts and associated processes. While the application of substantive legal rules to the particular facts of a case involves the processes of legal reasoning outlined in Chapter Two, the institutional handling of the case involves the issues we examine in this chapter.

Whereas the major distinction in substantive law is between public and private law, the only distinction in procedural law is between criminal and civil procedure. The former governs litigation concerning crimes, the latter regulates all other litigation.

The differences between criminal and civil procedure can be identified by at least five characteristics. First, the parties in criminal and civil cases are different: criminal cases are actions between the Crown and the accused, civil cases are between the plaintiff and the defendant. Second, the two kinds of cases begin differently: criminal cases start with a summons or arrest, civil cases with a statement of claim. Third, the two cases differ as to pre-trial proceedings: in many criminal cases there are preliminary hearings, in civil cases there are usually written pleadings. Fourth, and particularly important, there is a difference as to the burden and standard of proof: in criminal cases the burden of proof is on the Crown to prove the accused's guilt beyond reasonable doubt, whereas in civil cases the plaintiff, who usually bears the burden, only has to prove the case according to the balance of probabilities. Fifth, the objectives of criminal and civil trials are different: the objective of a successful prosecution is the punishment of the accused, the objectives of a successful civil suit are usually compensation for loss or harm.

I. CRIMINAL PROCEDURE

Crimes set out by Parliament, as well as provincial offences, are handled by the same procedure. The enforcement, application and administration of criminal law takes place mostly under provincial jurisdiction, although punishment of serious offences takes place mostly in federal institutions. The exact details of criminal procedure vary according to the category or classification of the offence.

A. Classification of Offences

For procedural purposes, offences fall into two main classes. One of these classes, consisting of indictable offences, can only be created by Parliament. The other, consisting of offences punishable on summary conviction, can be created both by Parliament and by provincial legislatures.

Originally the basic difference between the two classes of criminal offences was straightforward. The less serious offences, misdemeanours or what the *Criminal Code*[1] calls summary offences, were tried quickly (summarily) by magistrates or justices of the peace. The more serious offences, felonies or what the *Criminal Code* calls indictable offences, were preliminarily inquired into by the justices of the peace to test the validity of the charge (indictment) and then sent for trial by jury to a higher court by judges of what was usually called the King's or Queen's Bench.

This relatively clear distinction has been blurred by later developments, mostly in this century. Today, indictable offences in Canada are themselves subdivided into three sub-classes. First, there are the very serious offences in the *Criminal Code*, murder, sedition and conspiracy for instance, which must be tried by a province's superior trial court presided over by a federally appointed judge. Second, there are some indictable offences, theft under $1,000 for example, which must be tried by a provincially appointed magistrate or, what in some provinces is now called a provincial court judge, without a jury (the court structures and appointment of judges will be described in more detail in Chapters Six and Seven). Third, there are the remaining indictable offences that can be tried, at the option of the accused, by a magistrate alone or by judge and jury.

Summary offences, by contrast, form one single category. They must be tried by the magistrate or provincial court judge. Whether created by

---

[1]   R.S.C. 1985, c. C-46.

Parliament or by provincial legislatures, they constitute the least serious offences and carry a maximum penalty of six months' imprisonment or a fine of $2,000, unless otherwise provided in the statute creating them. Hybrid offences may be considered a third category, as offences which, according to the section of the Code creating them, may be tried summarily or on indictment upon the option of the Crown.

B. The Criminal Trial Process

1. COMMENCEMENT OF PROCESS

Although the criminal process may be said to commence the moment police inquiries begin, the formal commencement of process starts in one of two ways: (1) by arrest without warrant; or (2) by laying an information.

To arrest someone is to place them under a legal duty not to escape from the person arresting them. This may be done either by informing them that they are under arrest and getting them to submit or else by seizing them by force. In Canada citizens may arrest without warrant in certain circumstances, (*e.g.*, where a citizen finds a person committing an indictable offence). Police officers have much broader powers of arrest without warrant and can, for instance, arrest anyone whom they believe on reasonable and probable grounds to have committed an indictable offence.

As a result of the *Bail Reform Act*[2] police must not arrest an accused who can be brought to court by other means. They must not arrest for summary offences, hybrid offences or minor indictable offences where they have reasonable and probable grounds for believing that the public interest is served without an arrest. In considering the public interest they must take into account (1) the need to establish the suspect's identity; (2) the need to preserve evidence; (3) the need to prevent continuation or repetition of the offence; and (4) the likelihood that the suspect will appear in court. In such cases the police have two alternatives. They can let the suspect go, lay an information before a justice of the peace and apply for a summons. Or they can hand the suspect an appearance notice; a short ticket-like form indicating the offence alleged and requiring the accused to appear in court to answer the charge.

A police officer who does arrest must take the suspect before the officer in charge of the station. Officers in charge may take one of three courses: (1) release the suspect unconditionally if they believe there is no

---

[2]   S.C. 1970-71-72, c. 37.

danger to the public interest; (2) issue an appearance notice if the suspect promises to appear in court or enters into a recognizance (a formal written undertaking) so to do; or (3) hold the suspect and within 24 hours take the suspect before a justice of the peace.

Instead of arresting the suspect, the police officer may lay an information before a justice of the peace. This is a statement in writing and on oath alleging that the suspect has committed a specified offence. The justice must now issue a summons or a warrant for the suspect's arrest. A summons is an order to the accused informing him or her of the offence alleged and requiring appearance in court to answer the allegation. A summons must be issued unless the justice believes that the public interest requires the issuance of a warrant. A warrant is an order to the police within the jurisdiction of the justice, naming a certain suspect, describing the offence alleged and requiring them to arrest him or her for that offence. Such a warrant may be issued, for example, where an accused fails to answer a summons, to comply with an appearance notice, or to carry out a recognizance or promise to appear.

Another kind of warrant is the search warrant issued by justices to authorize search of buildings and seizure of things connected with, or evidence of, offences against the *Criminal Code*. Without a search warrant or writ, a police officer has no right in general to search anyone or anything, except for a common law right to search anyone lawfully arrested.

2. BAIL

There may be a considerable lapse of time between an accused's first appearance in court and the subsequent trial. In the interim, accused persons may be released on bail, that is, on their own assurance that they will appear for trial. This assurance may be required to be accompanied by a payment of money, by the deposit of a bond or by the surety of a friend.

Bail is directly connected to the venerable principle of *habeas corpus*. Trial should take place within a reasonable period or the accused should be given a reasonable opportunity for bail. The writ of *habeas corpus*, as it developed in late seventeenth century England, was a check against indefinite detention by authorities and was consequently held up as a constitutional guarantee of civil liberties. Although often suspended in colonial Canada, and sometimes after Confederation, under state security laws such as the *War Measures Act*,[3] the writ has been set out as a right under the *Bill of Rights* and *Canadian Charter of Rights and Freedoms*.[4]

Since the *Bail Reform Act*, bail *must* be granted in certain cases. Authorities are to grant bail for summary offences, minor indictable offences, hybrid offences and offences punishable by not more than five years unless the Crown "shows cause" why the accused should be detained. The Crown can do this by persuading the magistrate or justice of the peace that the accused's release will not be in the public interest or that the accused will not appear in court.

In certain cases, the burden of proof is reversed and bail will not be granted unless the accused shows cause why it should. Such cases relate to the commission of an offence while waiting for trial on another offence, to the commission of offences by persons not ordinarily resident in Canada and to the commission of certain offences under the *Controlled Drug and Substances Act*.[5] There are also certain offences for which bail can only be granted by a judge of the Supreme Court of the province. These offences include murder, hijacking an aircraft and acts of treason. Judges will exercise their discretion in these bail decisions, and must be aware that the writ of *habeas corpus* is available (unless suspended by explicit legislation) and and that trial must take place within a reasonable period of time (see sections 10 and 11 of the Charter).

3. FROM PRELIMINARY PROCEEDINGS TO TRIAL

After arrest, summons or appearance notice, the accused appears before the magistrate. It must then be determined whether the case is to be tried summarily or on indictment. Summary offences and minor indictable offences must be tried by magistrates, some indictable offences must be tried in higher courts, and some indictable offences may be tried either by the magistrates, or in a higher court by judge and jury, or by judge alone. For offences in this last class accused persons must be asked how they wish to be tried summarily or on indictment.

Summary offences, as explained earlier, may be either federal or provincial. The former are tried according to the procedure laid down in the *Criminal Code*, the latter according to that prescribed by the provinces, which have mostly adopted the Code procedure. In either case, the accused pleads guilty or not guilty there and then and is tried by the magistrate.

---

[3] R.S.C. 1985, c. W-2 [Repealed R.S.C. 1985, c. 22 (4th Supp.) s. 80].
[4] Part I of the *Constitution Act, 1982* being Schedule B to the *Canada Act 1982* (U.K.), 1982, c. 11.
[5] S.C. 1996, c. 19.

Indictable procedure is more complex. First there is a preliminary inquiry (which the defendant may waive in certain cases) before a magistrate to determine whether there is a *prima facie* case against the accused. At this inquiry witnesses for the prosecution will be examined, cross-examined and re-examined, and so, if the accused wishes, will witnesses for the defence. At the end of the inquiry the magistrate will either discharge the accused or commit for trial.

The second stage in procedure on indictment is the actual trial. Very briefly, this begins with the arraignment, when the accused is asked to plead guilty or not guilty (there are also various other technical please). Next comes the swearing of the jury, if there is one. After this, the prosecutor opens the case and calls witnesses, who are examined, cross-examined and re-examined. In turn, such witnesses as the defence decides to call (including the accused if an election to that effect is made) are examined, cross-examined and re-examined. Then the closing speeches of the defence and prosecution are made, usually in that order.

The trial then moves to the judge's summing up, which instructs the jury on the law and sums up the evidence for them. A judge must exercise care in this so as not to provide basis for a party to appeal. Next comes the verdict: in a jury trial the jury gives its verdict, which must be unanimous, otherwise the jury may have to be discharged and the trial reheard by a new jury. In a non-jury trial the judge gives the verdict and will usually give reasons for it.

The final stage involves a discharge if the accused is found not-guilty or the sentencing stage if the accused is convicted. Sentencing can be a lengthy process with submissions from the Crown, victims and defence. The judge usually has considerable discretion in handing out a sentence up to the maximum specified for the offence, but will take these submisssions into consideration as well as broader considerations such as deterrence and the offender's prospects for rehabilitation.

4. APPEALS

Since "to err is human," provision must be made for setting right unsatisfactory decisions in criminal cases. To meet this need, Canadian law provides a right of appeal against verdict or sentence for both the accused and the prosecution. Historically, appeals of criminal trials were rare because of great deference to the verdicts of juries and to the abilities of judges. Prosecutors have unusually wide rights of appeal in Canada, which perhaps also reflects the historical powers of the Crown in Canada and our deference to its authority. The Crown or public prosecutorial authority has limited or no right of appeal in most other common law jurisdictions, except with regard to stated cases.

For summary convictions there are two types of appeal. The first type is on grounds of error of law or excess of jurisdiction. Appeal lies from the magistrate or provincial court judge to a judge of the superior court. This may be by way of "case stated" where the magistrate is required to state a case for the superior court judge by setting out the decision and the reasons for it. Alternatively, appeal may be on grounds of law, fact, mixed law and fact or against the sentence where either side may appeal. Cases may be further appealed from a superior court to a provincial court of appeal, and from there to the Supreme Court of Canada.

Appeal lies directly to the provincial court of appeal for convictions on indictment. The accused may appeal as of right against sentence or on questions of law. In order to appeal on all other questions, the leave or permission of the appeal court or trial judge is necessary. Again, in what is a departure from most common law jurisdictions, the Crown has wide rights of appeal. It may appeal as of right on questions of law and with leave of the court of appeal against sentence. However, an appeal by the Crown against a jury acquittal can, if successful, only result in a new trial. An appeal court cannot substitute a conviction for an acquittal.

II. CIVIL PROCEDURE

All non-criminal cases, actions in contract or tort for instance, are regulated by the rules of civil procedure. These rules, developed over centuries by the common law, formed part of the law of the different provinces before Confederation. After Confederation, they continued to fall under provincial jurisdiction since they concerned matters of property and civil rights in the province.

In Canada, each province has rules of civil procedure governed by highly technical provincial legislation. Although such rules may vary from province to province, their basic framework is the same. Here we outline civil procedure in very general terms and provide occasional reference to the rules in Ontario.

Civil actions in the superior courts of a province have six general stages: (1) commencement of action; (2) pleadings; (3) discovery; (4) trial; (5) judgment; and, in some circumstances, (6) appeal. The first three stages are intended to clarify the issues between the parties, to establish whether there are sufficient grounds to warrant an action to be heard by a court, and to provide encouragement for the parties to settle before the trial begins.

THE CRIMINAL PROCESS

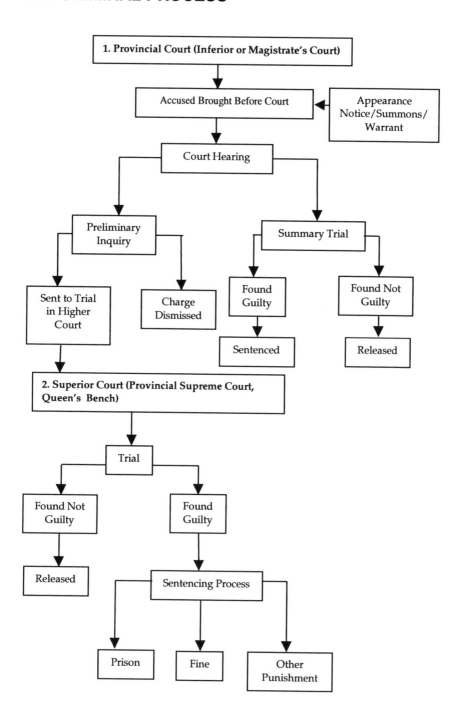

THE CIVIL PROCESS

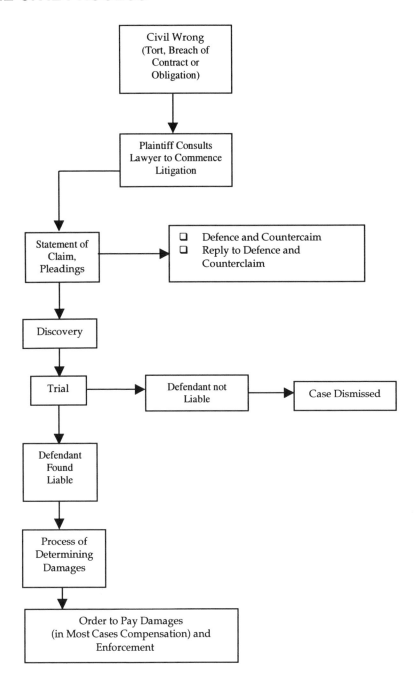

A. Commencement of Action

Most cases start informally with an exchange of letters between the parties or their lawyers. If, as the aggrieved party, you get no satisfaction and decide to sue, your first task is to get your opponent before the court. This is usually done, in most provinces, by a statement of claim. These have developed from the "writ of summons," a royal command to a named person compelling appearance to answer the specified complaint or suffer judgment by default. Writs played an important role in the history of common law, signifying the court's acknowledgement of a plaintiff's "cause of action," in other words, a complaint that warrants the court's attention. The merits of the case, of course, remain to be determined as the process moves to trial. Until this century, much of legal education centred on the study of the forms of action, writs, and pleadings, all of which involved bringing a dispute to the attention of a court and getting a court to act on it.

The writ of summons has been replaced by a simple statement of claim in many jurisdictions (in Ontario with the new *Rules of Civil Procedure*[6] in 1985). If for some reason there is insufficient time to file a statement of claim, the plaintiff may send the defendant a notice of action, a brief statement which informs the defendant that a claim is pending, summarizes the claim and must be followed within 30 days by a statement of claim. Nor does the defendant have to appear. The defendant simply files a defence to the statement of claim.

B. Pleadings

Pleadings are documents exchanged between the parties to determine the issues in dispute. They set out the facts on which each side relies. They begin with the statement of claim, in which the plaintiff's case is set out and the remedy requested. Then comes the defence in which the defendant answers the plaintiff's case. The answer may take the form of a traverse (denial of facts alleged) or a confession and avoidance (admission of the facts alleged and allegation of further facts exonerating the defendant). The answer may also include a counter-claim (complaint against the plaintiff and request for a remedy). Finally comes the reply (answer to the defence, denial of facts alleged by way of avoidance and defence to the counter-claim).

These different documents serve a variety of purposes. They determine the issues between the parties. They bind the parties. In an action

---

[6] R.R.O. 1990, Reg. 194.

pleaded simply for breach of contract, the plaintiff cannot claim, and the court cannot award, damages in tort. The documents also determine matters of evidence, such as which party has the burden of proof and what evidence can be advanced.

C. Discovery

Even after the pleadings, some issues may still be uncertain. Various procedures by way of discovery are available to prevent surprise at trial. Parties may interrogate their opponents before an officer of the court, and though the answers are not actually binding in court, the opponents cannot easily change their position at the trial. Parties may require opponents to produce documents in their possession and relevant to the case, may call for inspection of property involved in the suit and, in personal injury cases, may as defendants, have plaintiffs examined by experts such as impartial physicians. These procedures help to minimize bluff and posturing and encourage out of court settlement.

D. Trial

A civil trial follows many of the same patterns as its criminal counterpart. The plaintiff opens the case and calls witnesses, who are examined, cross-examined and re-examined. The defendant likewise calls witnesses, who are also examined in the same manner as the plaintiff's witnesses. Next, both sides address the judge or, in some rare cases, the jury. In Canada, the vast majority of civil cases that do not involve juries, the judge's decision follows. In a jury case, the judge summarizes and the jury enters a verdict.

E. Judgment and Execution

Judgments against a defendant fall into two categories: (1) orders to the defendant to do, or not to do, a certain act; and (2) orders to the defendant to pay money or hand over property to the plaintiff. Normally, the defendant will comply. Non-compliance with the first kind of order may result in imprisonment for contempt. Non-compliance with the second kind must be remedied by the plaintiff's levying execution (*i.e.*, initiating procedures for collection).

There are various methods of execution. The plaintiff may apply for (1) a writ of execution ordering the sheriff to seize the defendant's goods, sell them by public auction and pay the plaintiff's damages out of the proceeds; (2) a writ of possession, used for the recovery of land; (3) a writ of delivery, used for the recovery of specific goods or documents; (4) a charging order to be laid on bonds, stocks and shares which cannot be seized under a writ of execution; (5) the appointment of a receiver to hold the defendant's receipts from rents or interest payments; or (6) a garnishee order against money owing to the defendant (*e.g.*, wages) requiring it to be paid directly to the plaintiff.

F. Appeal

Either party may appeal the decision to the appeal court of the province and in certain cases there may be further appeal to the Supreme Court of Canada. Where a case has been tried by jury, the appeal court may order a new trial but will not normally do so unless there has been a miscarriage of justice. Where a case has been tried by judge alone, the appeal court may also order a new trial but will normally review the case itself on the basis of the transcript of evidence and draw its own conclusion.

III. EVIDENCE

The law of evidence is related to the law of procedure in that it helps to determine how a court will handle a dispute. In particular, the law of evidence regulates the admission and weighing of the factual details of a case, which together with the applicable substantive law, constitute the criteria the court considers to reach a decision. Put simply: Facts + Law = Decision (reached through the applicable procedural rules).

Evidence law consists of rules concerning witnesses, evidence and its admissibility, and burden of proof. These rules owe their development to common law but have now come to be regulated also by statute. Although common law continues to play an important role, evidence in criminal cases is partly governed by the *Criminal Code* and by the *Canada Evidence Act*,[7] while evidence in civil cases, being a matter for provincial law, is partly governed by the provincial Judicature Acts, Rules of Procedure and Evidence Acts. Here we shall confine ourselves to the most basic principles. There are numerous cases where the issues raised below are tested and elaborated.

A. Types of Evidence and Witnesses

Evidence can be distinguished in several different ways. One distinction is between oral evidence, documentary evidence and real evidence. The first two of these are self-expanatory; the third ordinarily

---

[7]   R.S.C. 1985, c. C-5.

refers to material objects such as the weapon in a murder case. Another is between direct evidence (*e.g.*, witnesses who testify they saw the accused kill the deceased) and circumstantial evidence (*e.g.*, evidence that the accused's fingerprints are on the murder weapon, that there are traces of gunpowder on his clothes, *etc.*)

To be a witness one must be competent. At one time, parties to an action, including the accused in criminal cases, were not competent and were debarred from giving evidence because they might be prejudiced in their own favour. Today the main example of an incompetent witness is a young child. When such a person is put forward as a witness, the judge will decide as a preliminary matter by examination whether the child has sufficient understanding to be allowed to testify.

Not all witnesses who are competent are compellable. A compellable witness is one who can be made, by subpoena if necessary, to give evidence. Today most witnesses are compellable. The main example of uncompellable witnesses are accused persons who cannot be made to testify against themselves.

The examination of witnesses follows a set pattern. First, the witness is examined by the lawyer who called the witness to the stand. At this stage, the examination-in-chief, the witness must not be asked leading questions. A leading question is one putting the answer in the witness's mouth. So, in a murder trial, the Crown Attorney must not say to his or her own witness, "Did you then see the accused rush into the room, pull out a gun and shoot the deceased dead?" If such questions were permissible, the Crown could in reality supply the evidence in the form of questions punctuated by the witness's occasional answer. Instead, the Crown must get witnesses themselves to tell their story and say what happened. Then the witness is tested by cross-examination by the other party's lawyer. Here attempts are made to query the accuracy of the witness's perception, correctness of recollection and in some cases veracity of evidence. Here, leading questions are allowed. If the defendant is going to put forward statements conflicting with the witness's, the defendant must put these statements to the witness so that the latter can try to deal with them.

The last stage is re-examination. The lawyer calling the witness puts questions about matters raised in cross-examination and attempts to repair any damage done to the case.

It should also be noted that under section 13 of the Charter, a witness who testifies in any proceedings has the right not to have incriminating evidence used against him or her in any other proceedings. Exceptions are made for perjury prosecutions and for the giving of contradictory evidence.

B. Admissibility of Evidence

The basic principle concerning admissibility of evidence is that all relevant evidence can and should be admitted and that no irrelevant evidence can be admitted. There are, however, some kinds of evidence which are not required and some which are not admissible.

In general, matters of fact can only be proved by evidence. Some matters, however, are so well known that no evidence is required to prove them (*e.g.*, the number of days in the week, the length of the period of gestation, the date, the name of the reigning monarch, *etc.*). On all these matters judges can rely on their own knowledge. As lawyers put it, they can take judicial notice.

Illegally obtained evidence, for instance evidence obtained by force without a warrant, may be ruled inadmissible. Section 8 of the Charter adds that that everyone has the right to be secure against unreasonable search and seizure.

Finally, there are some matters that may be relevant, but are nevertheless inadmissible. Indeed, much of the law of evidence consists of rules excluding various kinds of evidence from admissibility. The reason for these rules was that when they came into being, cases were mostly tried by juries, who, the judges feared, might through ignorance or prejudice attach undue weight to certain types of testimony. The three prime examples of such testimony are character, opinion and hearsay evidence.

1. CHARACTER EVIDENCE

In criminal cases the accused's bad character or previous convictions cannot generally be put in evidence. This, in a sense, is out of step with ordinary life. If I am considering hiring X as a cashier, it will be highly relevant if that person has been convicted frequently of stealing from his or her employer. Likewise, if a theft has been committed by X, Y or Z, it is obviously relevant to anyone making investigations that Y is a convicted thief. In strict logic, though, it does not prove Y was the thief on this occasion. Juries, however, are not always strictly logical but are liable to jump to conclusions. Hence the rule that unless accused persons "let their character in," by claiming they have a good character when they have not, or by attacking the character of the prosecution witnesses, no evidence of their bad character is admissible before conviction.

2. OPINION EVIDENCE

In general, witnesses' opinions are not admissible. Witnesses state facts and courts draw conclusions. This rule, however, has some exceptions. One concerns expert evidence. Often a court will have to decide whether two letters were written by the same person, whether the fingerprints on a murder weapon are those of the accused, whether the plaintiff in a personal injury case is liable to get better. Recognized experts are best able to pronounce on these matters. On such matters, then, experts are allowed to testify as to their opinions. The role of expert witnesses is an area of some controversy. Some argue that courts should be authorized to call in experts to clarify technical matters in issue where the litigating parties themselves fail to do so. Others argue that this inquisitorial type action has no place in an adversarial process of justice because of its potential to interfere with the rights of the parties.

A more straightforward exception to the opinion evidence rule relates to ordinary matters which are a mixture of fact and opinion. "The man was old," "the woman was tired," "the car was travelling fast," these and many similar propositions of everyday life are partly a matter of perception and partly a matter of judgment. As such, they are in general allowed in evidence.

3. HEARSAY EVIDENCE

The most famous of the exclusionary rules is that concerning hearsay evidence. According to this rule witnesses can only be called to say what they saw or heard and not what other people told them. So, in a murder trial X could be called to testify to seeing the accused shoot the victim but not to testify that Y saw the accused shoot the deceased. A witness is not allowed to advance someone else's statement as evidence of the fact stated.

Not that hearsay evidence is logically irrelevant. After all, if X heard Y claiming to see the accused shoot the deceased, this is some evidence against the accused. But not very strong evidence: Y, the original witness, not being on oath, may not have spoken seriously or sincerely and not being subject to testing by cross-examination may not have spoken accurately. A jury, however, might not realize these shortcomings and might perhaps attach undue importance to such hearsay evidence. For that reason it was excluded altogether by the common law.

Like almost every rule of law, the hearsay rule is subject to exceptions. The most important exception is an admission or confession by a criminal defendant. Though strictly hearsay, such confessions are admitted. Indeed, in the majority of cases they form the most significant evidence for the prosecution. However, admissions are not open to the objections generally made to hearsay evidence. True, the original witness was not on oath, but an admission of guilt is rarely made without seriousness or sincerity. True too, the witness was not made subject to cross-examination, but is now before the court and can clarify or otherwise correct the statement. Confessions may be questioned closely of course, particularly the circumstances under which they were obtained. Here the Charter has had an enormous impact not only on the methods police use to obtain physical evidence, but on the questioning of suspects as well (see sections 7 to 12).

Perhaps the most difficult aspect of hearsay evidence is that evidence can be hearsay without appearing so. Not all such evidence is in the form "X told me that..." It may look like a straightforward statement of fact. Take the following statements: "I am 19 years old, I was born in Ottawa, and I am the son of John and Mary Smith." All these are hearsay: the makers of such statements cannot vouch for them out of their own knowledge, they must rely on what parents and others have told them. Often a witness is allowed to put such statements in evidence because they are not particularly material to the case. Exceptionally, however, as might be the case in a charge of drinking under age, they might need to be properly established by production of a birth certificate, proof of identity and so on.

C. Burden of Proof

Evidence is weighed differently in criminal and civil proceedings, "beyond a reasonable doubt" in the former and on a "balance of probabilities" in the latter cases.

In criminal proceedings, the Crown has the burden of proof and the accused enjoys the presumption of innocence. This common law principle began to develop real meaning in the early eighteenth century as the increasingly frequent appearance of lawyers for the prosecution and accused demanded further articulation of the principle. By this century it became clearly established that the Crown must prove its case beyond a reasonable doubt. In some cases, the accused does not even have to answer the prosecution's case if this threshold is not established. Most cases are not so poorly-handled and the accused attempts to raise doubts about the liability or other important matters of evidence in the Crown's case. If the accused raises sufficient reasonable questions about these matters, the judge or jury are to give the accused the benefit of the doubt.

There have been exceptions in certain areas of the criminal law, such as the "reverse onus" provisions found in the *Controlled Drugs and Substances Act* and the *Official Secrets Act*.[8] Some of these have been challenged under section 11(d) of the Charter.

---

[8]   R.S.C. 1985, c. O-5.

The relatively high threshold of proof in most criminal proceedings reflects the fact that some of the most powerful forces of the state are arrayed against the criminal accused. Interestingly, lawyers in the eighteenth century looked to the procedural protections given the accused in cases under the *Treason Act*,[9] arguing that the the same civil libertarian protections should extend to cases involving more routine criminal offences.

Such concerns are not pressing in civil proceedings. Here, the plaintiff merely has to prove his or her case on a "balance of probabilities." This simply means something more than 50 per cent likely or passing the threshold from what is plausibly possible to what is persuasively probable. Defendants do not receive the same benefit of doubt as the criminal accused.

Many of the procedural issues raised in this chapter are rather technical in nature. However, it is important to keep in mind that they lie at the core of what are essentially process questions. Matters such as access to justice and legal aid, the role of legal counsel and police procedures form an important practical context to procedural law. They are examined in more detail in Chapter Seven.

The law of evidence is also best understood in context. Our adversarial system of justice, which has existed for centuries with the common law, means that the disputing or litigating parties are the motor force of trial proceedings. They are seen to be the primary sources of evidence. The judge may rule on questions of admissibility and will determine whether there is sufficient proof (except in jury trials). For a judge to independently introduce evidence, however, is seen to be contary to our common law system, an "inquisitorial" innovation that can threaten the rights of the parties. Some of the American legal realists introduced in Chapter One argued that such principle has little connection to what happens in practice. The litigant with the most resources tends to be the party that wins the battle of proof. They also point out that best proof is not necessarily the same as the truth. In adversarial systems, proof is usually a mere approximation of the truth when the sole sources of evidence are the parties themselves.

---

[9] (U.K.), 1695, 7 & 8 Will. III, c. 3.

FURTHER READING

V. Del Buono, ed. *Criminal Procedure in Canada* (Toronto: Butterworths, 1982)

P. Fitzgerald, *This Law of Ours* (Scarborough: Prentice-Hall, 1977)

A.J. Meagher & R.A. Meagher, *Civil Procedure Simplified* (Toronto: Butterworths, 1983)

G. Parker, *An Introduction to Criminal Law* (Toronto: Carswell/Methuen, 1987)

C.M. Powell, *Arrest and Bail in Canada*, 2nd ed. (Scarborough: Butterworths, 1976)

J. Sopinka, S. Lederman & A.W. Bryant, *The Law of Evidence in Canada*, 2nd ed. (Toronto: Butterworths, 1999)

G.D. Watson, S. Borins & N.J. Williams, *Canadian Civil Procedure: Cases and Materials*, 2nd ed. (Scarborough: Butterworths, 1977)

Chapter Six

The Courts and Other Forms of Dispute Resolution

The courts are the central institution of our legal system, yet most disputes are not resolved by the courts of law. While growing problems exist with court back-logs and delayed justice, largely a result of Canada becoming increasingly litigious, most disputes are in fact settled before they get to court. Many are resolved informally or through negotiation involving lawyers under the shadow of litigation (including criminal cases when plea bargains are concluded). Alternative forms of dispute resolution have become increasingly popular.

Adjudication, the resolution of disputes through a decision of a court of law, achieves an authoritative settling of issues between the parties, a definitive determination of their practical rights and obligations, and, ideally, a result that accords with justice. On the other hand, it is a process that is costly and time-consuming. As we saw at the end of Chapter Five, our courts rely on an adversarial procedure, a sort of "battle" where the disputing parties are the "motor force" of the trial process. One party wins the battle and the other loses. The need to present the dispute adversarially and the win/lose outcome may not always be appropriate. This is especially the case where the parties are in a continuing relationship, where fault is difficult to allocate, and compromise is the most equitable solution.

The structure of courts in Canada is complex. Courts are organized according to the role of the federal and provincial governments in their operation, to jurisdiction (where and what matters the courts are entitled to adjudicate), and to their position in the court hierarchy (the flow of authority between courts examined in the discussion of precedent in Chapter Two).

I. A MIXED COURT SYSTEM

Canada's court system is based on the English system of courts, modified by federalism, which results in a court structure that is in some ways similar to that of the United States of America. As a unitary state, England has inferior (county and magistrates') courts to handle minor matters, superior courts (high court with Queen's bench, chancery and family divisions) for the trial of more serious matters, a single national court of appeal, and the House of Lords, which is the final court of appeal for the whole country. As a federal state, the United States has two parallel, independent sets of courts in addition to local inferior courts: state supreme courts and courts of appeal for matters falling within state jurisdiction and law, and federal district courts and courts of appeal for matters involving federal jurisdiction and law. The United States Supreme Court serves as a final court of appeal for both the state and federal courts.

Canada's system largely replicates the basic English structure of inferior and superior trial courts and two appeal courts, but has adapted it to a federal state structure. Three important provisions of the *Constitution Act, 1867*[1] affect the organization of Canadian courts. First, section 92(14) of the Act gives responsibility for the administration of justice in each province to each respective provincial legislature, reflecting the fact that well-established court systems based on the English model existed in provinces before Confederation. Second, section 101 of the Act authorizes the Parliament of Canada to establish a court of appeal and any additional courts needed for the better administration of Parliament's laws. Third, sections 96, 99 and 100 of the Act give the Parliament of Canada the power to appoint, pay and dismiss judges of the higher provincial courts. The federal government appoints judges to the superior courts of the province, to the provincial courts of appeal, and to the Supreme Court of Canada, which is the final court of appeal for the entire federation. The provinces appoint judges or magistrates to the inferior courts. We will examine questions of judicial appointment and review of their performance in Chapter Seven.

As a result of these constitutional arrangements, our court system has several distinctive features. First, most matters arising under federal or provincial law are dealt with by courts that are administered by the provinces. These courts have remained largely as they had been when the province entered Confederation. Unlike the United States, there is no distinction between the courts that try matters of federal law and those that try matters of provincial law. Second, the judges of these courts may

---

[1]   (U.K.), 30 & 31 Vict., c. 3, reprinted in R.S.C. 1985, App. II, No. 5.

be federally — or provincially — appointed. The seriousness of the matter determines whether a case goes to a superior court for trial before a federally-appointed judge. Third, all appeals from provincially appointed courts, including matters of provincial law, are heard by federally-appointed judges. However, superior and provincial appeal courts are administered by each province while the Supreme Court of Canada is administered by the federal government.

There is yet another factor that adds to the complexity of Canada's court structure. Federal and provincial governments have set up courts to handle matters that are seen to be too specialized for regular civil and criminal proceedings. So, for instance, the federal government has created the federal court for the trial and appeal of administrative law disputes and tribunal decisions under its jurisdiction. Many provinces have created specialized family courts, usually as a branch of the regular courts.

II. JURISDICTION

A court's jurisdiction is its authority to hear, adjudicate and give decisions and in Canada such authority now derives from statute. The provincially administered courts are regulated by provincial legislation such as the Judicature Acts, the Provincial Court Acts, the Small Claims Court Acts and so on. The federally administered courts are regulated by the federal *Supreme Court Act*[2] and the *Federal Court Act*.[3]

Legislation may define a court's jurisdiction in various ways. It may define jurisdiction in terms of the law to be administered, with the most basic and common being the division between criminal or civil matters. It may define jurisdiction geographically, so that a court can only try disputes arising in a particular area or occurring between parties residing in a particular area. Or, legislation may define jurisdiction in monetary terms by reference to the amount of money claimed or the value of the property in dispute.

The legislation that creates and administers a court will specify whether it is a superior or inferior court and whether the court is one of "record" with powers to fine or imprison for contempt of court. Lower level or inferior courts have geographically and monetarily limited jurisdiction. In contrast, the superior courts have largely unlimited jurisdiction, although

---

[2] R.S.C. 1985, c. S-26.
[3] R.S.C. 1985, c. F-7.

such a court will not have jurisdiction in matters where its judgement cannot be enforced (*e.g.*, over criminal offences committed outside the province or over disputes concerning title to land outside the province). Beyond this, no matter is in principle beyond the jurisdiction of a superior court. Its judgements cannot be challenged in any collateral court, although they can be reversed by a higher court of appeal. An inferior court is one whose proceedings can be stayed, reviewed and quashed by higher courts, is generally not one of record, and its officers are not protected from liability.

III. A PROVINCIAL EXAMPLE: COURT HIERARCHY IN THE PROVINCE OF ONTARIO

While the general four-level organization of inferior and superior trial courts and two appeal courts applies across Canada, trial courts have been combined and divided in different ways and use a bewildering array of names (some use English names, others American, and still others have created new terminology) so that further generalization about court hierarchies in each province is difficult.

As noted earlier, trial courts and provincial courts of appeal are an exercise of provincial jurisdiction over the administration of justice under section 92(14) of the *Constitution Act, 1867*. Each province and territory is responsible for designing its own court system. Although each system is unique, and provinces use different names and divisions for their courts, the differences are minimal in practice. Extensive court restructuring has recently taken place in the Province of Ontario and we turn to it as our example.

For some time there had been three levels of trial courts or "courts of first instance" in Ontario, including middle level county courts, which have recently been subsumed into the superior courts. Currently, the Trial Court of Ontario (formerly the Ontario Court of Justice) consists of the following divisions:

CIVIL LAW COURTS: ONTARIO COURT STRUCTURE

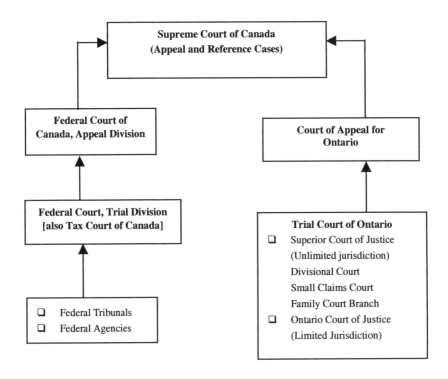

CRIMINAL LAW COURTS: ONTARIO COURT STRUCTURE

A. Superior Court of Justice
(formerly the Ontario Court [General Division])

This court has jurisdiction over all indictable offences, trying cases by judge and jury or judge alone, as elected by the accused. Under section 469 of the *Criminal Code*[4] certain serious offences (most notably murder) must be tried by this court. This court also hears most civil cases in its various divisions. The Family Court Branch (formerly the Unified Family Court) has exclusive jurisdiction over certain family law matters (*e.g.*, divorce). It also has jurisdiction over persons prosecuted under the *Young Offenders Act*[5] if the court is present in the area where the offence was committed.

B. Ontario Court of Justice
(formerly the Ontario Court [Provincial Division])

This court shares jurisdiction over criminal law matters involving adults with the Superior Court of Justice under section 553 of the *Criminal Code*. In practice it tries less serious cases and as many as 90 per cent of criminal offenders are actually tried by this court before a judge. The court also has jurisdiction over youth and family matters. Persons prosecuted under the *Young Offenders Act*, except in those parts of the province served by the family court branch of the Superior Court of Justice, will appear in this court. In addition, the court deals with family law matters, except those reserved to the Family Court branch of the Trial Court of Ontario by the *Courts of Justice Act*[6] (*e.g.*, divorce).

C. Court of Appeal for Ontario

The provincial appeal court is known as the Court of Appeal for Ontario. The court consists of a chief justice, an associate chief justice and 14 other judges. Appeals to this court can involve either civil or criminal law matters and are heard by a panel of at least three judges. Lower court decisions of the Ontario Court of Justice may first have to be appealed to the Superior Court of Justice before they can be appealed to the Court of Appeal for Ontario.

---

[4] R.S.C. 1985, c. C-46.
[5] R.S.C. 1985, c. Y-1.
[6] R.S.O. 1990, c. C.43.

IV. FEDERAL COURTS

As we have seen, the *Constitution Act, 1867*, provided that existing provincial courts would continue to function after Confederation, and that they would enforce laws falling under federal jurisdiction and passed by the Parliament of Canada. Hence, the Parliament of Canada did not require any courts other than the courts existing in the provinces to make its laws effective. It simply added responsibilities to those courts. However, section 101 of the *Constitution Act, 1867*, did authorize Parliament to establish an appeal court for Canada and any additional courts for the better administration of the laws of Canada.

It was not until 1875 that Parliament established the Supreme Court of Canada as an appeal court of civil and criminal jurisdiction for the entire country. Until then appeals proceeded directly from provincial appeal courts to the Judicial Committee of the Privy Council in England. As we saw in Chapter Three, the Privy Council remained the final court of appeal for Canada in criminal cases until 1933 and in all other cases until 1949.

The Supreme Court of Canada is composed of eight justices and a chief justice. Three members of the court must have been members of the bench or the bar of Quebec. In addition, convention holds that three judges should be from Ontario, one from British Columbia, one from the prairie provinces (either Alberta, Manitoba or Saskatchewan), and one from the Atlantic provinces (either New Brunswick, Newfoundland, Nova Scotia or Prince Edward Island). Quorum of the court is five justices, but important constitutional questions are usually heard by all nine members.

There are some statutory rights of appeal, for instance where there is a dissenting judgment on a question of law in criminal cases in a provincial appeal court. However, appellants usually need the court's permission (leave to appeal) in order to proceed. Leave is granted where the court deems a criminal or civil case as involving matters of public importance. Applications for leave to appeal are heard before three judges in civil cases and five in criminal matters. The Supreme Court of Canada also hears appeals from the appeal division of the Federal Court of Canada

The Supreme Court has an important additional function. It hears reference cases directly. Any question of law or fact may be referred to the Supreme Court by the federal government, through the office of the Governor General of Canada. Most reference cases are constitutional in nature, involving questions of the division of powers and authority of the federal and provincial governments.

Parliament also established the Exchequer Court in 1876, a court of first instance with limited jurisdiction involving largely Crown revenues and maritime law. In 1970, the Exchequer Court and other smaller federal courts and tribunal appeal boards, were absorbed into the new Federal Court of Canada. Matters were made more complex again in 1983 when Parliament transformed the Tax Review Board into a separate Tax Court of Canada.

The Federal Court consists of a trial division and an appeal division, with a chief justice, an associate chief justice and 29 other judges. In addition to the jurisdiction of the former Exchequer Court, the Federal Court has jurisdiction over intellectual property matters of copyright, trademark and patents; administrative law disputes involving the actions of federal employees; and appeals from some boards and tribunals. The appeal division hears appeals from the trial division and appeals directly from select federal boards and tribunals (*e.g.*, the Immigration Board, the National Parole Board and the Tax Court of Canada).

V. CANADIAN COURTS:
FEATURES AND ISSUES

As we have seen, cases are presented and proceeded adversarially in Canada. It is argued that that such a procedure, where there is minimal judicial intervention, best ensures the rights of the disputing parties. On the other hand, as we saw at the end of Chapter Five, "best proof" is not the same as the "truth." Moreover, the effectiveness of one's case depends on good research and advocacy. These usually require considerable resources, including a good lawyer. We will examine problems of access to the courts in Chapter Seven.

Other features of Canada's courts are formality and public openness. The costumes of the judges and lawyers, the forms of address and the special rituals of the proceedings are designed to evoke the majesty of the court and the solemnity of its deliberations in the search for justice. Canadian courts have preserved the traditional English legal forms to a greater extent than American courts. Many argue that these forms lend greater dignity to Canadian courts. Such symbols of British justice also speak to the role of order in Canadian political culture historically, serving as a positive point of difference from American frontier justice. Others argue such traditions make the proceedings more remote, especially for minority cultures.

For the most part our courts are open to the public, a constitutional guarantee that dates back to the Glorious Revolution, 1689 and before.

However, in certain situations proceedings may be held *in camera*. National security under the *Official Secrets Act*[7] proceedings may be a pretext for closing proceedings to the public. *Young Offenders Act* proceedings may also be closed when in the opinion of the judge it is in the public interest to do so. There is also a publication ban in such proceedings, based on the argument that the public stigma of proceedings should be lessened in the case of youths. Publication bans can be extended to adult criminal proceedings, and bans are routinely in place when it comes to naming the accused in preliminary proceedings, and in exceptional cases in the trial itself, as was recently seen in the case of the Paul Bernardo video tapes.[8] These limits on public openness are contentious and have, in some cases, been challenged under the Charter, so far unsuccessfully.

Despite the finality of the decisions of courts, and the general public deference to them, courts can make mistakes, despite the availability of appeals. The wrongful murder convictions of Donald Marshall, David Milgaard, Guy Paul Morin and recent questions about the murder convictions of Steven Truscott and Robert Baltovich remind us of the fallibilty of our courts. Section 690 of the *Criminal Code*, where the Minister of Justice may consider an application for the Crown's mercy and order a new trial or re-examination by an appeal court, has not proved to be an effective way of correcting such injustices.

Canadian courts are primarily oriented to compensation in the case of civil proceedings and punishment in the case of criminal proceedings. They are not terribly effective at achieving conciliation. Moreover, they are costly and slow. Delays in the administration of justice have been challenged under section 11(b) of the Charter. The best known case involving the right to be tried in a reasonable time is *R. v. Askov*,[9] where the Supreme Court of Canada held that a number of circumstances will be taken into account, including the length of delay, the explanations for delay and prejudice to the accused.

There have been a number of responses, including, not surprisingly, calls for more resources for courts and Crown prosecutors. Perhaps the most dramatic response has been the rise of alternative dispute resolution.

---

[7] R.S.C. 1985, c. O-5.

[8] *R. v. Bernardo* (1994), 121 D.L.R. (4th) 212 (Ont. C.A.).

[9] [1990] 2 S.C.R. 1199.

VI. ALTERNATIVE DISPUTE RESOLUTION (ADR)

Increasingly, persons involved in disputes and legal conflicts are looking beyond the traditional court structure, particularly to avoid the cost, which is particularly important when they are in ongoing relations with the other party and conciliation or compromise is the most desireable result. Governments and justice officials have also embraced ADR in an attempt reduce public spending, and to clear case back-logs. ADR has become very common in family law disputes. It has even extended to criminal cases, where there is increasing use of diversion for first time and young offenders in particular, and to increased involvement of the community in formulating a response.

The formal alternative dispute resolution models fall into four categories:

A. Negotiation

Those in conflict are encouraged to resolve the problem by more effective communication. A forum is provided for the parties to meet with one another or they may choose to send a representative to speak on their behalf.

B. Mediation

A neutral third party, or mediator, is asked to meet with the parties and to help them resolve the conflict. The mediator's job is to help the parties come up with options that will allow them to freely agree to a settlement that satisfies their needs. The mediator cannot make a decision for the parties, instead, he or she will help the parties to decide what solution works best for them.

C. Conciliation

The process of conciliation looks a lot like mediation. For example, the mediator has to be neutral and he or she cannot tell the parties what decision to make. As a result, people often confuse the two processes. However, conciliation is distinct from mediation in that the conciliator plays a larger role in the process than the mediator. Conciliation is often used when the parties are not able to work together in the same room. Often, the conciliator will meet with each disputant separately and then present their point of view to the other party. Sometimes conciliators will listen to what everyone has to say and then write an advisory report saying what they think the parties should do to resolve their dispute. When this is done the parties can choose to: (1) accept the report; (2) use the report as a starting point for further discussions; or (3) ignore the report.

D. Arbitration

The process of arbitration looks a lot like adjudication, although like the other forms of ADR it aims for a compromise result rather than a win or lose outcome. A neutral arbitrator holds a hearing and then issues a ruling in much the same way as a judge would. Arbitration also differs from adjudication in that the parties get to choose: (1) whether to use arbitration as a way to settle their differences; (2) who the arbitrator is; and (3) whether the arbitrator will make a binding decision, or merely issue an advisory opinion.

THE CONFLICT RESOLUTION CONTINUUM

	Alternative Dispute Resolution: Negotiation, Mediation, Conciliation, Arbitration	Adjudication
Outcome	Compromise	Win/Lose
Third Party Intervention	Decreases	Increases
Disputing Parties	More Control	Less Control

Whether or not the above features of the different forms of ADR are considered advantages or disadvantages depends largely on who you are asking. For example, some people think that the fact that ADR tends to be more informal than adjudication is an advantage. They argue that all of the rules that go along with using the court system can prevent the parties from reaching a settlement that works well for them. However, others argue that those legal rules are essential because they prevent more powerful parties from taking advantage of less powerful parties by forcing them to agree to a settlement that is not in their best interests. There is also disagreement over whether the fact that ADR tends to occur in private is a good thing. Supporters of ADR argue that private mediation of divorce disputes is best because it allows families to avoid having their "dirty laundry" aired in public. Critics counter by saying that some matters considered behind closed doors (*e.g.*, spousal or child assault) should be dealt with in a public courtroom in order to confront the matters effectively.

There is disagreement over whether ADR is cheaper and faster in the long run than adjudication, particularly when agreements cannot be enforced. Some even argue that ADR is just a way for the government to force people to pay for costly alternatives to a publicly subsidised court system. There is little doubt that lawyers have become increasingly interested in ADR and debate is heating up over what qualifications are necessary for its responsible practice.

There are no easy solutions to the problems we face with dispute resolution. ADR and other means of diversion from the courts are not a cure-all. There are advantages and disadvantages to litigation and adjudication in the courts as well as to the alternatives. If conflicts cannot be prevented by other means then the most effective means of dispute resolution depends very much on the nature of the conflict. In the end, our courts have the final say. It is there that our rights and responsibilities are most authoritatively determined.

FURTHER READING

L. Boulle & K. Kelly, *Mediation: Principles, Process, Practice* (Toronto: Butterworths, 1998)

R.A.B. Bush & J.F. Folger, *The Promise of Mediation* (San Francisco: Jossey-Bass, 1994)

G. Gall, *The Canadian Legal System*, 3rd ed. (Toronto: Carswell, 1990)

B. Laskin, *The British Tradition in Canadian Law* (London: Stevens, 1969)

R. Martin & G.S. Adam, *Sourcebook of Canadian Media Law*, 2nd ed. (Ottawa: Carleton University Press, 1996)

S. Roberts & M. Palmer, *Dispute Processes: ADR and the Primary Forms of Decision Making* (London: Butterworths, 1998)

P. Weiler, *In the Last Resort* (Toronto: Carswell, 1974)

Chapter Seven

People in the Legal Process

The law and its processes involves a great variety of people. This chapter includes a survey of the personnel of law (judges, the jury, police and other legal officials), citizens who use the law and lawyers who represent them. The issues concerning these people are wide-ranging and particular to each group. We introduce some of them in each of the sections that follow.

I. CITIZENS AND ACCESS TO JUSTICE

Citizens have input into the shaping of law in many different ways. They participate in the election of members of Parliament and the provincial legislatures, who in turn generate laws through legislation. Citizens act as plaintiffs and defendants in civil cases, and may become an accused or a victim in criminal cases. They may also act as witnesses in these proceedings, and form the jury in cases where one is required. Citizens are involved in the law in less formal ways as well, for example, in community watch schemes where they are asked to play a role in the prevention of crime.

All citizens also have equal rights of access to justice, at least in theory. As we noted in the previous chapter, however, practical access to the courts usually demands both time and resources. The affluent in society are invariably in the best position to take advantage of the courts to vindicate their rights. For this reason, there are various initiatives to create more equitable access to justice.

Legal aid and community law clinics are two important services available to the the less affluent in society. Legal aid is state-subsidised legal service provided by a lawyer who is usually in a regular practice. It is available to people who are unable to pay but qualify for the service. Community law clinics are staffed by lawyers who specialize in the types of legal problems typically faced by the poor. They are joined by other specialists, such as social workers, and the clinic is administered by representatives from the community served.

Legal aid and community law clinics are discrete services. In legal aid, the services are similar to those provided for regular paying clients, whereas in community law clinics there is a recognition that the legal problems faced in a particular community may be unique, requiring services unlikely to be required by paying clients.

There are other initiatives that are designed to encourage greater use of legal services. Although arguably aimed at increasing access to justice, their most important function is to stimulate the market for legal services. Innovations in the charging of fees and advertising are examples. They represent a departure from the traditional view that entrepreneurial activity is below the professional dignity of lawyers.

Contingency fees, where a lawyer has a speculative interest in the outcome of the case (charging nothing if it is lost and a percentage of the award if it is won), have long been used in the United States and are now allowed in some Canadian jurisdictions. Restrictions on lawyer advertising have been recently relaxed in most Canadian provinces. Another innovation is pre-paid legal service plans, which work along the lines of dental and health insurance plans. Such plans are increasingly requested in collective agreements and employment contracts.

II. LAWYERS

In the common law provinces (*i.e.*, all provinces except Quebec) all lawyers are sworn in as both barristers (who traditionally had the exclusive right to appear in court) and solicitors. It is a "combined bar" whereas traditional English practice is to keep functions of solicitors (lawyers who deal with legal matters outside of court) and barristers (lawyers who appear in court) separate. Other branches of the profession, such as attornies, disappeared at the end of the eighteenth century, although the term is widely-used for lawyers in the United States, and has been retained in Canada for limited use when referring to lawyers acting on behalf of the Crown in criminal prosecutions. Lawyers translate client problems into legal language, process documents, provide counsel on legal matters, and act as advocates on behalf of clients in court.

In Quebec the profession remains divided into *notaire publiques* and *advocats*. The notaries' main function is drafting contracts and authenticating them in a manner required by the *Civil Code of Quebec*,[1] conveyancing, and acting in non-contentious matters where neither law nor facts

---

[1] S.Q. 1991, c. 64.

are in dispute. The advocat represents clients in court, similar to the barrister, but is also involved in practically all other spheres of legal activity, including work of the notaires.

Whether in Quebec or in the other provinces, lawyers have a threefold responsibility. First, their duty is to their clients, who are entitled to have their cases properly considered, prepared and presented. Second, they owe a duty to the court, of which they are all officers. Third, they have a broader public responsibility to society to comply with ethical standards in the practices of their profession.

These duties may conflict. Criminal defence lawyers are often asked how they can defend an accused they know to be guilty. The answer is that guilt can only be determined by a court of law and that they are responsible for ensuring that their client has the full benefit of his or her rights. On the other hand, witholding evidence in certain circumstances on the basis of the client's rights (as in the case of the Paul Bernardo video tapes), may conflict with the lawyer's ethical responsibilities, duty to the court and the integrity of the process of justice.

Each province has passed legislation to regulate the practice of law within its jurisdiction, and each has a professional governing body (usually called law societies) to ensure these legal rules are complied with. The law societies set further detailed regulations for professional practice on matters such as advertising and fees, discussed above. They also set the requirements for admission to the practice of law, including professional education and qualification standards (see Appendix B, Legal Education and Becoming a Lawyer). The provincial law societies also handle complaints of malpractice and the disciplining of members who have been found to violate the rules and regulations.

The legislation of professional standards is in the public interest. However, there is professional autonomy in the enforcement of standards. Self-regulation is premised on the view that professional peers are in the best position to evaluate whether standards are adhered to. As with other modern professions, these very features also mean that the established profession tends to claim monopolistic powers over practices that come within its area. Conflicts over the role of paralegals and unresolved issues about the degree of involvement and control by lawyers over alternative dispute resolution reflect these tendencies. On the other hand, it is argued that it is in the public's best interest for lawyers to have final responsibility for contentious legal matters, at least.

In many areas, however, the work of lawyers and others who deal with the law is complementary. Lawyers are assisted both in private practice and elsewhere by non-lawyers who are nevertheless experienced or

trained, usually in community college programmes. These paralegals include professional title searchers, legal aid assistants, law clerks and legal
secretaries. They perform many of the same legal functions as lawyers,
except that restrictions have been placed on giving legal advice, undertakings, appearing in court. The lawyers employing them remain ultimately responsible for their activities. These restrictions are under
challenge, particularly by many paralegals who work independently of
lawyers.

Other issues facing the profession include the current over-supply of
lawyers and the challenges facing law firms by internationalization and
mergers. The growth of "mega firms" has created real difficulties for
smaller non-specialized firms in urban areas. Although women now
make up over half the number of law students and graduates, the profession remains highly stratified, particularly at the senior partner level.
These and other issues may lead to further changes to the legal profession.

III. JUDGES

Judges are the presiding officers in the courts. Their function is to hear
cases, determine issues and give decisions according to the law contained
in precedents and legislation. As we saw in Chapter Three, the judiciary
functions as the third branch of the state, ensuring the integrity of the rule
of law by functioning independently of the legislative and executive
branches.

The formal guarantees of judicial independence are security of tenure
and the separation of powers. These guarantees emerged relatively recently in the history of the common law system. They were the result of
long struggles against the political manipulation of the courts. For instance in the early seventeenth century, Francis Bacon argued that the
judge's first duty is to the king while Sir Edward Coke argued that the
judge's first duty is to the integrity of the law. The experience of the
Court of Star Chamber and political trials suggest that Bacon's view prevailed in the short term only. Security of tenure, meaning that judges hold
office according to good behaviour determined by Parliament rather than
the according to the pleasure of the Crown, was achieved in England at
the time of the *Act of Settlement, 1701*[2] and in Canadian jurisdictions at

---

[2]   (U.K.), 12 & 13 Will. III, c. 2.

the time of the *Constitution Act, 1867.*[3] The exclusion of senior judges from the direct involvement in deliberations of government cabinets was achieved in the first half of the nineteenth century in both England and Canada.

These formal guarantees of judicial independence are elaborated in modern legislation, notably the federal *Judges Act*,[4] which specifies what judges can and cannot do while in office, and by the function of the Canadian Judicial Council, a peer body of senior judges, which issues advisories on matters not clearly stated under the Act. The council also hears complaints about federally appointed judges, disciplines or issues warnings to them when warranted, and in extreme cases of judicial misbehaviour, prepares recommendations to Parliament for dismissal (judges are otherwise entitled to hold office until the age of 75). Judges are removed by the Governor General on address of the Senate and House of Commons. Provincially appointed judges may be dismissed by the Lieutenant Governor after an inquiry.

As noted in Chapter Six, the *Constitution Act, 1867* gives the federal government the power to appoint judges to the Supreme Court of Canada, provincial courts of appeal and superior trial courts and to the Federal Court of Canada. The provincial governments appoint judges and magistrates to the inferior courts.

The formal guarantees of judicial independence are better described as protections than guarantees. For instance, they do not preclude partisanship in the appointment of judges. Until the 1950s many of the judges appointed to the Supreme Court of Canada had no prior judicial experience and a good number were prominent lawyers who earned their position by being active in governing party politics. This, as much as continuing appeals to the Judicial Committee of the Privy Council, undermined the credibility of Canada's highest court. Nor do the formal guarantees of judicial independence address the fact that judges may have political influence within their appointed function in the courts. This has been a growing concern, particularly since the advent of the Charter, about judges' widening influence on public policy.

For these reasons there have been calls for reforms to the way judges are appointed. Federally appointed judges are recommended by the Minister of Justice, who invites candidates amongst lawyers of good standing (upon recommendations and in consultation with the Canadian Bar Association and provincial law societies) or from judges who have distin-

---

[3] (U.K.), 30 & 31 Vict., c. 3, reprinted in R.S.C. 1985, App. II, No. 5.
[4] R.S.C. 1985, c. J-1.

guished themselves in the lower courts. A list is forwarded to cabinet and the Privy Council, and then on to the Governor General. Provincial appointment processes are similar although some initiatives have been taken to broaden the pool of candidates by creating advisory committees.

There have also been proposals to make judicial appointments more open and accountable at the federal level by having candidates reviewed by all-party parliamentary committees. In the United States, some state judicial positions are elected and proposed senior federal appointments are reviewed by congressional committees. There is debate about the advantage of such processes. While they may be more democratic, they also have the effect of making appointments more partisan. There is little doubt, however, of the importance of having a judiciary that is both highly capable and representative of social diversity, especially given its ever-increasing impact on public policy.

IV. THE JURY

The jury originated in medieval England and retains an important role in Canada's legal system. The jury in adversarial proceedings displaced the ancient procedures of trial by battle and trial by ordeal. The process developed by entrusting the verdict of guilt or innocence to "twelve men good and true," prominent local figures who were in a position to arrive at a decision on the basis of the facts as presented by the parties, their own knowledge of local circumstances and the law as instructed by the presiding judge.

In later years, jurors became more broadly representative of the community and the factual circumstances for their consideration were limited strictly to the evidence put before them. This was achieved in the nineteenth century after long struggles against "jury-packing" (the selection of biased jurors) and the linking of jury qualification to sufficient property ownership.

Jury selection today can be a complex, long and drawn-out process. During the process by which members of the jury are chosen before the trial begins, the lawyers for the Crown and the accused have the opportunity to ask potential jurors questions to determine their suitability. If it is felt that the juror may be biased as to the outcome of the case, or if the juror appears to have knowledge of the case beyond what one would expect in an ordinary citizen, then either side may prevent the person from serving on the jury. This is called a challenge. The Crown and defence will exploit this opportunity (the Crown has the right to more challenges than the defence) in the attempt to select jurors who are most sympathetic to their respective positions.

The right to trial by a jury of one's peers has long been regarded as an important constitutional liberty. Juries are a "lay presence" in the administration of law. More particularly, jury nullification of law, or the exercise of its "verdict according to conscience," has historically served as a popular check on oppressive laws and prosecutions. Juries arguably still serve as such a check as demonstrated in the trials and appeal to the Supreme Court of Canada in the Morgentaler abortion cases.[5] The jury acquittals, despite clear guilt on the facts, reflected the perceived injustice of the abortion law as it then stood.

Although less than 10 per cent of criminal trials in Canada involve juries today, trial by jury still tends to take place in the most prominent and contentious cases. Cases of murder and treason are tried by jury, and the accused can elect trial by jury for most other serious offences. The judge decides questions of law and summarizes the evidence heard in court in his or her instructions to the jury on how to proceed. These instructions, called the charge to the jury, must be carefully crafted or they can serve as grounds for appeal and re-trial. It is up to the jury to decide which version of the facts is most compelling and to apply the law as described by the judge in reaching its verdict.

Juries in civil cases are even more rare than in criminal proceedings, although either side may request one. Even where statute requires a jury (*e.g.*, in cases of libel or slander), it may be dispensed with if both sides agree. Civil juries are more common in the United States and many argue that they contribute to the inflation of damage awards.

Jury composition differs in criminal and civil cases. Criminal juries consist of 12 members, except in the Northwest Territories, where six is the rule. Civil juries vary but consist of six in Alberta, Ontario and Quebec. A criminal jury must give a unanimous verdict, but a civil jury may give a majority verdict. Jury qualifications are laid down in detail by the Jurors Act in each province. In general, jurors must be over 18, citizens of Canada, free from conviction for an indictable offence and lacking physical or mental incapacity. In addition, certain people are exempt from jury duty (*e.g.*, members of Parliament or of a legislature, judges, lawyers, students-at-law, clergy, medical practitioners and police officers).

The question of the jury's value has long been debated. Critics of jury trials stress the inexpertness of the jurors, the possibility of emotion triumphing over law, and the dangers these uncertainties pose to the

---

5   *R. v. Morgentaler*, [1988] 1 S.C.R. 30 at 76.

rule of law, in particular, to equal treatment under the law. The reduction of the role of the jury in England and Canada has reflected further utilitarian considerations such as the extra time involved and the burden of jury service on the citizen. Champions of the jury point to its historical role and its continuing importance as a means of ensuring citizen participation in the processes of the law and keeping the law in tune with community sentiments.

V. OFFICERS OF THE CROWN

A. The Attorney General

This ancient office originated in the sovereign's practice of appointing lawyers to represent the Crown in the various courts. The Attorney General was the chief law officer of the Crown who, in turn, could appoint deputies. Today, the Attorney General of Canada or of a province is a cabinet minister, member of Parliament or of a legislature, appointed by the Crown on the advice of the Prime Minister or provincial premier. Attorneys General are almost always lawyers but rarely represent the Crown in court. In Canada the federal Minister of Justice also holds the title of Attorney General of Canada.

Though politicians, Attorneys General, as chief law officers of the Crown, are also public officials. They supervise the public prosecution of criminal offenders. They also exercise prerogative powers, including "preferred indictments", which eliminate preliminary hearings and "stays of proceedings", which withdraw prosecutions. These powers are justified on the basis of public interest in speedy and reputable justice. Attorneys General also act as legal advisers to the government. It is to the Attorneys General that we look for the vindication of public rights, enforcement of criminal law, and the suppression of excessive or oppressive exercise of power by tribunals, boards and other public bodies. In all these functions they must exercise a degree of independence quite different from that required of other members of cabinet.

Attorneys General, then, act in a dual capacity. They are both politicians participating in forming governmental policy and official guardians of public rights. As a result, they can be faced with conflicts of interest. Their role in supervising the prosecution of political offences or crimes generating political controversy is particularly sensitive. Another source of potential conflict arises out of the Attorney General's simultaneous position as legal adviser to the government and to Parliament. Parliamentary convention holds that there is no obligation to divulge to Parliament legal advice tendered to the government, and in general law officers' opinions are not made public. Opinions requested by either House of Parliament, however, are made public.

B. The Solicitor General

The office of Solicitor General came into being in fifteenth century England as a deputy of the Attorney General. While some provinces have discontinued the office others have retained it, usually with supervisory responsibility over policing and provincial correctional institutions. The federal Solicitor General is a minister of the Crown who heads government departments concerned with the Royal Canadian Mounted Police, the Canadian Security Intelligence Service, the Correctional Service of Canada and the National Parole Board.

C. Crown Attorneys

While criminal prosecutions are the ultimate responsibility of the Attorney General, in practice they are conducted by their agents, called crown attorneys. Regular lawyers specially briefed are also sometimes retained to act on behalf of the Crown. The provinces have legislation that details the organization, function and responsibilies of crown attorneys.

D. Crown Solicitors

Crown solicitors are the legal officers who conduct the non-criminal legal business of the Crown. In the federal government, these are all officers of the Department of Justice assigned to various departments. In the provinces there is no fixed pattern: some departments have their own legal staff while others use lawyers from the Attorney General's department.

VI. ADMINISTRATIVE OFFICERS OF THE COURT

A lawyer taking a case to court comes into contact with a number of officials and other administrators concerned in the operation of the courts. These include masters, registrars, court clerks, sheriffs and bailiffs. They ensure that writs and warrants are produced and served for the commencement of proceedings and the obtaining of evidence, that the courts function according to proper procedures and that judgements of the court are enforced.

Justices of the peace are some of the most important of these officials. They are appointed by the Lieutenant Governor of a province on the advice of the Attorney General. Historically, they were prominent citizens of the community who served as the government's local administrative representatives and were in charge of running the local courts. They also served as magistrates presiding over the trial of minor criminal offences. Their judicial function has been largely displaced by provincial court judges, but they still try a small range of summary conviction offences under the provincial judges' supervision. These offences include Liquor Act offences, minor tax offences, Traffic Act offences and infringements of municipal bylaws. Justices of the peace continue to play a vital function in taking criminal informations, issuing summonses and warrants and granting bail.

VII. THE POLICE

The police are primarily responsible for the enforcement of criminal law. Their functions include keeping the peace and maintaining law and order by being a visible presence in communities; arrest and investigation; and a wide range of related matters such as responding to complaints, resolving disputes, road traffic management and front-line social services.

Professional policing is a comparatively recent development in the Canadian legal system. Until the nineteenth century, English communities and colonial Canadian settlements relied upon community peace officers under the supervision of the justice of the peace. These officers included parish constables and the night watch-men. The militia would be called in to deal with rioting or other forms of disorder that were beyond the capacity of this rudimentary public system of law enforcement. A mounted paramilitary police force, the Royal Irish Constabulary, was set up by Sir Robert Peel after the Irish Rebellion of 1798. Despite long-standing calls for reforms to law enforcement in urban centres, professional policing was resisted by many who viewed it as as a tyranical European innovation that threatened traditional British liberties. It was only in 1829 that professional policing was instituted in England, beginning with Peel's Metropolitan London Police.

Policing in Canada reflects the tradition of the "blue" (Peel's London Police) and, in the case of the Royal Canadian Mounted Police, the tradition of the "brown" (Peel's Irish Police). All large cities and many smaller ones have their own city police, and Ontario and Quebec have provincial forces responsible for law enforcement outside the cities. The Royal Canadian Mounted Police (RCMP) is the country's most prominent police force. The mounties, who played a central role in the development of the Canadian west, enforce particular areas of federal law generally, and, by contractual arrangement with provinces other than Ontario and Quebec, handle law enforcement in those jurisdictions where there are no urban forces. Most police forces have a uniformed branch for law enforcement and a plain clothes investigative branch.

As the front line of law enforcement, and possessing formidible powers to affect citizens' liberties, the police tend to bear the brunt of public controversy around the legal system. Shortcomings in the handling of complaints has led to civilian review processes in some provinces. Police misconduct and systemic problems sometimes require investigations by outside police agencies and even government inquiries. Such external review is sometimes resented by police officers, whose work is difficult and dangerous. However, most would agree that the rule of law is best ensured by highest standards of professionalism, public service and effective accountability. The recent proliferation of private security firms reflects the limits of police resources and raises concerns about standards of professionalism and accountability even more acutely.

Sir Robert Peel recognized that effective policing demanded winning the confidence of the community served. In the mid-twentieth century American-influenced "emergency response" models of policing had some impact on police practices in Canada. In recent years there has been a return to community-based models that attempt to reconnect the constable on the beat to the neighbourhoods policed.

FURTHER READING

B.K. Cryderman, A. Fleras & C. O'Toole, *Police, Race and Ethnicity*, 3rd ed. (Toronto: Butterworths, 1998)

G. Gall, *The Canadian Legal System*, 3rd ed. (Toronto: Carswell, 1990)

J.A.G. Griffiths, *The Politics of the Judiciary*, 2nd ed. (London: Fontana, 1981)

D. Lundy, ed., *Barristers and Solicitors in Practice* (Toronto: Butterworths, 1998)

Law Reform Commission of Canada, *The Jury in Criminal Trials* (Ottawa: Working Paper 27, 1980)

W.R. Lederman, "The Independence of the Judiciary" (1956), 34 Canadian Bar Review 1158

Peter H. Russell, *The Judiciary in Canada: The Third Branch of Government* (Toronto: McGraw-Hill Ryerson, 1987)

P.C. Stenning, *Appearing for the Crown: A Legal and Historical Review of Criminal Prosecutorial Authority in Canada* (Cowansville: Brown, 1986)

Chapter Eight

Law, Rights, Reform and the Future

Important as it is to understand substantive law, procedure and evidence, and the institutions and personnel of law, the subject of law cannot be adequately understood simply in terms of its technical aspects. The law is a means of finding solutions or resolutions for human problems and disputes. The law is also an authoritative state practice that shapes and regulates social relations and conflicts. The issues surveyed in the each of the previous chapters reveal controversies that cannot be resolved by simple technical means.

Contract law struggles to find a balance between commercial interests and those of consumers. More generally there are often huge distances between the promise of the law respecting remedies for wrongdoing in civil proceedings and what the law actually delivers. Criminal law involves complex conflicts between the rights of the victims and those of the accused. It also reveals broader tensions between public interest in safety and the prevention of harm and libertarian concerns about the power of the state. Constitutional law raises complex and political questions about the rule of law and the law-making powers of legislatures and judges.

There are no absolutely right answers to these sorts of problems. Only better and worse answers, and what is better at one place and time may well be worse at another. Law, no less than life, is not arithmetic. And life, as the American Supreme Court Justice Oliver Wendell Holmes once put it, is painting a picture, not doing a sum. Like any artist, legal artists must struggle against the limitations of their chosen medium.

The law has many limitations, and three in particular warrant mention. First, there is always a conflict between the demands of the particular case and the requirements of the general rule. Justice dictates that like cases be treated alike, and the same rule be applied to all, but no two situations are ever quite the same, and circumstances alter cases. Second, there is constant tension between law and reality. After all, laws are made in answer to problems raised by past experience. Tomorrow's problems may not be best resolved using yesterday's solutions. Third, (and this results from the previous two conflicts) in law there is an ever-present pull between the spirit and the letter. The need for fairness and justice calls for principles, ideals and values; the need for certainty and uniformity requires rules and rigid, abstract concepts.

The limitations of law also have a bearing on how much we can rely upon law for solutions. What are the limits and possibilities of progress through the law? A related question is posed by social scientists: does the law lead or follow social change?

Jeremy Bentham, introduced in Chapter One, had an optimistic view of the progressive potential of legislation. In Bentham's utilitarian world, economic efficiency, sensible governance and the greatest happiness for the greatest number could be achieved, so long as archaic and discretion-filled common law was swept aside wherever possible by legislation. Karl Marx shared some of Bentham's distain for established practices but his view of law's potential was entirely different. For Marx, law was a mere reflection of existing social relations. It leads only in the sense that it is an instrument of dominant class interests.

A balanced interpretation of historical experience would suggest that the law both leads and follows, and that it reflects both consensus and privilege. Certainly the medieval institutional developments under Edward I had enormous political, social and economic consequences. The eighteenth century common law innovations of English Chief Justice Mansfield greatly facilitated capitalism and industrialization. The sweeping legislative reforms of the nineteenth century both improved social conditions and expanded the reach of the state. The law was not the cause of these changes but it was an important institutional means of managing them and facilitating yet further change.

This complex picture colours any careful response to specific questions about the prospects of law — its limits and possibilities as an agent of progressive change and transformation. There are two basic areas of reform potential that we can explore for more specific answers to the question; reform through legislative processes and reform through rights struggles in the courts.

I. LEGISLATIVE LAW REFORM

Legislative law reform, which Bentham enthusiastically promoted and the state embraced in the nineteenth century, is ultimately a reflection of the struggle for change through our established political institutions. The law-making powers of Parliament and provincial legislature involve the democratic opportunities provided by these institutions and the advice offered to governments by the state's supporting bureaucracies.

As we saw in Chapter Two, there are a number of sources of legislation. Many bills arise out of the governing party's policies as announced in election platforms and the speech from the throne when legislative sessions begin. Occasionally a private member's bill will arise out of the advocacy of single elected representatives. Many bills also arise out of the advice offered to governments by ministries and departments or in response to the recommendations of royal commissions and inquiries. The policy branch of the Department of Justice, for instance, updates legislation and engages in legislative housekeeping.

The problem with these sources of legislation is that they are either a result of partisan party politics or are simply random responses to problems that have developed. Law committees and *ad hoc* royal commissions emerged in the nineteenth century to take a more comprehensive approach to legislative law reform but their mandates were limited.

A new kind of entity has emerged in years since World War II: the law reform commission. England, Scotland, Ireland, Australia, New Zealand and Canada (as well as a number of Canadian provinces) have established law reform commissions although they may not all be designated by this term. Unlike royal commissions and law committees, they are permanent bodies that are capable of taking a comprehensive approach and keeping laws continuously under review. They operate at arms-length from party politics and government departments and are staffed by independent specialists and consultants.

The Law Reform Commission of Canada was first established in 1971 and did much in its 21 years of existence to chart a new path in law reform. Three aspects of its approach are noteworthy. First, on the basis that a law is what it does, the commission concentrated not just on law in the books but on law in action, based on studies of what police officers, lawyers or judges actually do. Second, on the ground that what ultimately counts is principle, the commission strove to get beyond the technical details of the law and find its moral and philosophical underpinnings. Finally, on account of the peculiar division of powers in Canada, the commission realized that successful law reform in Canada is less a matter of altering legal rules than of persuading those applying these rules to change their ways and attitudes. In other words, improvements in criminal law would come not so much from changing the *Criminal Code*[1] as

---

[1] R.S.C. 1985, c. C-46.

from getting police, prosecutors, defence counsel, judges, prison officers, parole officers and others to do things differently. This being said, the commission also made a number of important specific proposals to change laws, notably its 1987 report recommending a new *Criminal Code*.[2]

The Law Reform Commission of Canada was abolished in 1992, along with a number of "independent" agencies, obstensibly as a cost-cutting measure. A scaled-back version of the Law Reform Commission of Canada has recently been established: the Law Commission of Canada. The new commission has attempted to confront the criticism of the old commission by avoiding overlap with the work of law and policy branches of government departments and by greater consultation with grass-roots social movements.

II. RIGHTS STRUGGLES

Reform through rights struggles in the courts is necessarily incremental. The courts deal with individual disputes on a case-by-case basis. However, their decisions can be precedents and victories in the courts can have great social symbolic value. Court decisions not only change individual and social behaviour, but they can change the actions of the state, notably through the *Canadian Charter of Rights and Freedoms*,[3] as well as the conduct of public and private institutions, as in the case of human rights proceedings.

Rights struggles have a long history in the common law system. Canadians did not suddenly acquire rights with the Charter in 1982. Before the Charter, rights derived from precedent, legislation, constitutional settlements and the more abstract formal claims that surrounded the rule of law. Particular Canadian rights, such as language rights and denomination school rights, were elaborated in the *Quebec Act, 1774*[4] and the *Constitution Act, 1867*.[5] The *Bill of Rights* articulated many of these existing rights. The contribution of the Charter to this history is the introduction of a powerful new means of enforcing these rights.

---

[2]   Law Reform Commission of Canada, *Recodifying Criminal Law* (Report No. 31) (Ottawa: 1987).

[3]   Part I of the *Constitution Act, 1985* being Schedule B to the *Canada Act 1982* (U.K.), 1982, c. 11.

[4]   (U.K.), 14 Geo. III, c. 83.

[5]   (U.K.), 30 & 31 Vict., c. 3, reprinted in R.S.C. 1985, App. II, No. 5.

It is also important to note that not all of our rights are found in the Charter, although Charter decisions attract the most current attention and debates. International human rights and federal and provincial human rights codes are also important contemporary sources of rights which involve separate processes for their vindication.

Rights may be placed into four broad categories: (1) political liberties (*e.g.*, freedom of expression); (2) legal liberties (*e.g.*, freedom from arbitrary arrest or detention); (3) egalitarian liberties (*e.g.*, right to be treated equally without discrimination); and (4) socio-economic rights (*e.g.*, social and cultural dignity and economic freedoms). In Canada, these rights are protected by the *Constitution Act, 1867*, the *Canadian Bill of Rights*,[6] the *Canadian Charter of Rights and Freedoms*, the *Canadian Human Rights Act*,[7] the provincial and territorial Human Rights Codes, and various international human rights treaties (*e.g.*, the Optional Protocol to the International Covenant on Civil and Political Rights), which Canada has agreed to observe.

A. International Protection of Human Rights

The treatment of the Jewish people and other civilian groups by the Nazis during the 1930s and 1940s has led to a heightened realization that there are standards below which no state must be allowed to fall in the way it deals with those that reside in its territory. Since World War II, national and international instruments have come into force aimed at ensuring that all states respect adequate standards of human dignity.

In 1948, the United Nations proclaimed the *Universal Declaration of Human Rights*. Although non-binding, this declaration remains an important statement of international ideals. This proclamation was followed by the *Convention on the Abolition of Forced Labour* (1957) and the *International Convention on the Elimination of all Forms of Racial Discrimination* (1965).

The first comprehensive, binding agreements appeared in 1966. These were the *International Covenant on Civil and Political Rights*, the *International Covenant on Economic, Social and Cultural Rights*, and the *Optional Protocol to the International Covenant on Civil and Political Rights*. These treaties impose a duty on the parties to ensure by legislation and other methods that the basic rights and freedoms of the individual are maintained. Canada has been bound by these agreements since

---

[6] S.C. 1960, c. 44.

[7] R.S.C. 1985, c. H-6.

August 19, 1976, but has been found to be in violation of them on more than one occasion. Generally, however, Canada has played a leading role in the development and implementation of these aspects of international law and in the international protection of rights (notably through international peace-keeping). Recent examples include the *Ottawa Accord on Anti-Personnel Mines* and the work of Madame Justice Louise Arbour, now of the Supreme Court of Canada, as chief prosecutor for the International War Crimes Tribunal.

B. Human Rights in Canada's Federal and Provincial Laws

Unlike the Charter of Rights, which is constitutionally entrenched through the *Constitution Act, 1982*,[8] the *Canadian Bill of Rights* is simply federal legislation which has served as a guide to the interpretation of federal laws. There has been little success with its use as a basis of challenging state laws and actions. The Charter has created the real means of such challenges.

While the Bill of Rights articulates rights and freedoms, it does not deal directly with remedies for discrimination and discrimination itself. It must be remembered too that the Charter only concerns the laws and actions of the state, and does not address the question of rights between private individuals or between individuals and private institutions. The provinces and the Parliament of Canada have enacted Human Rights Codes that address these gaps. The codes follow the same general pattern: certain discrimination is prohibited, a human rights commission is established, and procedures are laid down for dealing with violations of the code.

The Ontario *Human Rights Code*[9] provides a good example. Part I of the code provides for freedom from discrimination. It forbids discrimination against, or harassment of, people because of race, ancestry, place of origin, colour, ethnic origin, citizenship, creed, sex, sexual orientation, marital status, same-sex partnership status, family status, handicap, and in certain cases, age, the receipt of public assistance (*e.g.*, welfare), or record of offences (*e.g.*, criminal record). Discrimination is forbidden in areas including the provision of services, accommodation, contracts, employment and membership in associations based on any of the above-mentioned criteria.

---

[8] Being Schedule B to the *Canada Act 1982*, (U.K.), 1982, c. 11.
[9] R.S.O. 1990, c. H.19.

Parts III and IV lay down the composition and duties of the Ontario Human Rights Commission and enforcement procedures. Its duties are to promote public understanding and acceptance of the code, to conduct research, and to implement educational programmes designed to eliminate prohibited discrimination. Any person discriminated against can complain to the commission, and in certain cases the commission or one of its officers must investigate the matter and try to bring about a settlement. Failing a settlement, the commission may recommend that the Minister appoint a board of inquiry which will decide whether there has been a contravention of the Code and, if so, what steps the offender must take to put things right.

C. The Canadian Charter of Rights and Freedoms

We have examined the development of the Charter and its operation in detail in Chapter Three. Through the review process set out in section 1, the Charter asks the courts to evaluate whether there is a reasonable balance between enforcing respect for rights and broader public interests. If a federal or provincial government wishes to disregard a court's ruling (*e.g.*, that the measure is unconstitutional because there is no reasonable balance), it can include a notwithstanding clause under section 33 which preserves a democratic check on the courts' power, according to our constitutional tradition of parliamentary supremacy.

The Charter's association with the patriation of Canada's constitution has lent it a great deal of popular symbolic importance, although as we have seen it is only one source of rights in Canada. It has become the most prominent source because it is a constitutionally entrenched rights document with an explicit procedure that enables individuals or groups to challenge alleged rights violation by the state in the courts. It has also had the effect of significantly increasing the public policy role and political profile of the courts.

Judicial interventions in striking down democratically enacted legislation, including judgments that effectively re-write legislation through interpretation, have provoked controversy. Although judges are accountable to higher courts, the Supreme Court of Canada is not, and appeals are not the same thing as democratic accountability. Some critics argue that the circumstances under which the notwithstanding clause (section 33) can operate should be clarified so that it can be used more frequently. The powers taken on by the judiciary have also led to calls for reforms to the methods of appointing judges. On the other hand, supporters of the Charter argue that it has introduced a new dialogue between the courts and legislature, one that has improved the quality of our laws.

There is yet another concern. As we saw in the previous chapter, not all citizens have equal access to the courts in practice. As one critic of the Charter has pointed out, like the Ritz Hotel, the courts are open to all, so long as one can pay the costs. Charter challenges are expensive and the rights that tend to get vindicated are the rights of those who can afford it. This has caused further debate about the need for state subsidies to support Charter challenges and the status of "intervenors", interested groups who seek to support or challenge the party initiating the Charter case.

Has the Charter shifted more public policy powers to an unelected legal elite? Has it shifted important matters of public concern into the less accessible forum of the courts? Or is it a progressive change, one that not only improves the quality of laws and state actions by obliging the state to be more careful about rights, but also makes the law a more effective means of progress? It is probably too early to tell.

What the future holds for legislative reform and reforms through rights struggles remains to be seen. Our historical experience with legislation and court decisions gives us some idea of the progressive limits and possibilities of the law. The track record is a decidedly mixed one

At the same time, it is not necessary for us to approach issues in the same manner as we have in the past. As we saw in Chapter Two, Canada's legal system is the product of a particular culture, the institutional outcome of British colonial development and subsequent political events after Confederation. Our adversarial approach to justice, for instance, which poses a trial as a battle between the two contestants of whom one must win and one must lose should not limit our outlook on the future of dispute resolution.

Ultimately, our aim should be to minimize the intervention of law by minimizing the existence of disputes and conflicts. The law will nonetheless always remain, or at least until human nature and political life changes fundamentally. It reflects the dominant principles and interests in society, establishing and enforcing the rules all in society must follow, from the most disadvantaged to the most powerful.

Legal Research

A lawyer, said King George III, is not one who knows the law but one who knows where to find it. As we saw in Chapter Two, the primary sources of law are cases and statutes. These are the primary sources that lawyers rely upon in negotiation and litigation and judges rely upon to authoritatively resolve disputes.

How does one go about tracking down these sources to research a legal problem? There are a number of excellent legal research books and manuals, some of which are listed below. Although legal research is rather technical in nature, some brief general observations may be made. Legal research consists of three basic steps: categorization, familiarization, and investigation:

I. CATEGORIZATION

Legal problems are not clearly labelled contract, tort, and so on. Instead, lawyers attach these labels to cases because the law is organized into these different compartments. Before looking up anything, a lawyer has to know which compartment to investigate. In order to categorize along these lines, one needs a general grasp of law. (Chapters Three through Five provide a start, and reference to the Additional Readings sections at the end of these chapters enable a researcher to develop a general grasp of different areas of the law). An example: Karen goes to a stamp auction. The bidding for one of the items has reached $100, and the auctioneer says, "Does anyone bid $120?" Karen waves her catalogue to fan herself, and the auctioneer cries, "Sold to the woman at the back." Does Karen have to purchase the stamp? Karen would start by researching AUCTIONS, which would lead her to SALES, which in turn falls under CONTRACT, a matter of provincial law.

II. FAMILIARIZATION

Having located the specific area, one needs to develop a sense of the basic principles, the fundamental concepts, the special terms and the workings of that branch of law. Again, this book provides a start, but reference to a specialized text on the specific area of law will be necessary. Continuing with the above example, a law textbook on contract would give the researcher an idea of the principles concerning offer, acceptance, consideration, and so on. Scholarly articles constitute another important secondary source which can be accessed using the *Index to Canadian Legal Periodical Literature*.

III. INVESTIGATION

When researching a specific problem, in most cases one is better off beginning with secondary materials (*e.g.*, to see if there are references to the more specific matter of bids and auctions) rather than turning immediately to the primary materials (case and statute law). One can then proceed to legal encyclopedias and digests which are reference tools for cases and statutes. For instance, a widely used source is *Halsbury's Laws of England*. Refer to **Auctions** and **Contract** and check the *Halsbury's Laws of England — Canadian Converter* to these Volumes for differences in Canadian law. Note any relevant case or statute. Next, consult the *Canadian Encyclopedic Digest* (Ontario) or (Western) as the case may be, and note any relevant case or statute. Then consult the cited law reports (*e.g.*, Dominion Law Reports, Supreme Court Reports, provincial reports) and statute books (*Statutes of Canada*, provincial statutes) for the full text of actual cases and acts. Finally, check, with the help of index and statute citators, whether the relevant cases have been recently cited, distinguished, affirmed, followed, reversed or overruled, and whether the relevant statutes have been amended or repealed. It should also be noted that many reports and digests are now available on CD ROM and that research online, using computerized data bases such as Quiklaw and LEXIS-NEXIS, has revolutionized legal research, allowing for rapid access to the most recent cases.

As we saw in Chapter Two, the court's *ratio decidendi* (the core principle, the rule by which the case is decided) may be difficult to identify. This is particularly the case where there are multiple judgments (dissenting judgments do not qualify although they may point to where the legal principles remain uncertain and flexible). Headnotes or summaries provided at the beginning of the case provide some assistance. However, they should be used cautiously as they are not always sufficiently comprehensive or fully representative of the decision. The practical reach of legislation cannot be understood by simply reading the act in question. The researcher must also examine how the courts have interpreted the act, the circumstances in which it is interpreted according to its broad purposes, or alternatively, according to its narrow literal words.

While it is important to have a good grasp of the technical law, it should also be emphasized that researchers with broader questions about the role of law will not, in most cases, find sufficient insight from the sources described above. Interdisciplinary legal research involves a broader range of sources, borrowing from the research methods familiar to scholars such as social scientists and historians. Government documents, the archival records, qualitative and quantitive studies of institutional and social behaviour contain important additional insights into the origins of laws, administrative policies, how the legal system works in practice, and how people actually experience the law.

The sort of research required depends on the sort of research question formulated. In professional practice, the object is the resolution of a dispute where the sources are necessarily limited so that there can be an authoritative settling of a problem. Here, it is imperative that the researcher gets the technical law right. In scholarship, especially that which is not directed to professional practice, the object is to develop a better understanding of law's interactions with other institutions and with society. While it remains important to get the law right, the research exercise is necessarily wider-ranging.

SECONDARY RESEARCH MATERIALS OVERVIEW

Technical Law Secondary

M.A. Banks, *Using a Law Library: A Guide for Students in the Common Law Provinces of Canada*, 3rd ed. (Toronto: Carswell, 1991)

D.T. MacEllven & M.J. McGuire, *Legal Research Handbook*, 4th ed. (Toronto: Butterworths, 1998)

J.A. Yogis, I.M. Christie, M.J. Iosipescu & M.E. Deturbide, *Legal Writing and Research Manual*, 5th ed. (Toronto: Butterworths, 2000)

Dictionaries, Digests, Encyclopedias

Canadian Abridgement
Canadian Encyclopedic Digest, 3rd ed.
Halsbury's Laws of England (with *Canadian Converter*) 4th ed.

Osborn's Concise Law Dictionary, 7th ed. (London: Sweet & Maxwell, 1983)

D.M. Walker, *The Oxford Companion to Law* (Oxford: Clarendon, 1991)

Interdisciplinary Research

Consultative Group on Research and Education in the Law, *Law and Learning: Report to the Social Sciences and Humanities Research Council of Canada* (Ottawa, 1983)

T.B. Dawson, "Legal Research in a Social Sciences Setting: The Problem of Method" (1992), 14 Dalhousie Law Journal 445

M. Galanter, "Notes on the Future of Social Research in Law" in L. Freidman & S. Macaulay, eds., *Law and the Behavioural Sciences* (Indianapolis: Bobbs-Merril, 1977)

J. Hagan, "The New Legal Scholarship: Problems and Prospects" (1986), 1 Canadian Journal of Law and Society 35

P.H. Russell, "Overcoming Legal Formalism: The Treatment of the Consitution, the Courts and Judicial Behaviour in Canadian Political Science" (1986), 1 Canadian Journal of Law and Society 5

Appendix B

Legal Education and Becoming a Lawyer

There are basically four steps to becoming a lawyer:

1. Obtaining a law degree (LL.B. or B.C.L. in civil law jurisdictions);
2. Completion of articles;
3. Successful completion of Bar Admission Course and bar examinations; and
4. Admission to the bar.

The first step falls under the jurisdiction of the professional law schools. The other three fall under the jurisdiction of the provincial law societies described in Chapter Seven.

There is no pre-law course of study. Most professional law schools recommend a background in university studies that include social sciences and humanities courses where reading, writing, reasoning and analytical skills are developed. A number of Canadian universities offer undergraduate legal studies. These are, for the most part, inter-disciplinary programmes or courses that serve as adjuncts to other fields such as criminology, sociology, political science, business and public administration. Many provide insight into the importance of law as a social institution and practice, the relationship of the legal system to other institutions of the state, and the legal dimensions of human rights and public policy. Community colleges also offer law courses, usually of a more practical or applied nature, serving as backgrounds for paralegal practice, policing and private security.

None of these courses or programmes provide professional legal qualifications and no credit is given for them at professional law schools. While there is no such thing as a pre-law course of study, university undergraduate legal studies courses may give students a better idea of law, helping them decide whether to train to be lawyers. They may also provide some familiarization with the technical aspects of law, although it should be emphasized that educators at professional law schools are wary of incoming students carrying pre-conceived ideas and generally assume that the technical aspects of law must be learned from scratch.

Professional legal education is oriented towards technical vocation-training. Law, of course, is not just for lawyers. Undergraduate legal studies courses and programmes provide a foundation for examining this important social practice from the perspective of related fields. Graduate legal studies programmes, quite separate from professional law school studies, are beginning to emerge in Canada and reflect a scholarly orientation to the study of law.

The most important factor in professional law school admissions is grades. All Canadian law schools require students to have completed at least two years of recognized undergraduate degree studies, although most students are admitted after completing a pass or honours degree. Current admission statistics indicate the need for at least a good B+ (75 to 79 per cent) in university studies.

The second most important factor is the required Law School Admission Test (LSAT). This is a general knowledge test developed by the Law Schools Admission Services in the United States and is designed to measure the candidate's aptitude for the study of law. Whether the test accurately measures such abilities is open to debate, but the test has been widely embraced beyond the U.S. as a common measure for admission purposes. Tests are held four times a year at various centres in Canada. A free booklet describing the test and containing an application form can be obtained from the Pre-Law Advisor (LSAT) at most Canadian universities or by writing to: Law Services, Box 40, 661 Penn St., Newtown P.A. 18940-0998, U.S.A. The *LSAT Registration and Information Book* contains a limited amount of information on the programme and admission requirements of each Canadian law school. A poor test result will not necessarily preclude admission to law school, although a much higher academic average will be required. Conversely, a low academic standing could be offset by a very high LSAT score. The precise weighting given to the LSAT and the averaging of various attempts at the test varies from one law school to another.

Letters of recommendation may make a difference to an admissions committee, although most successful candidates are admitted simply on the basis of grades and LSAT result. Such a letter may be important if it serves to explain interruptions in an applicant's study programme (*e.g.*, on account of illness) or if the applicant has been in a field related to the study or practice of law.

Law schools in the Maritimes and Western Canada tend to give priority to applicants from their own province by means of an out-of-province quota. A number of Canadian law schools also set aside a small portion of admissions for candidates who qualify as mature students (the applicants must be in their late 20s and have been in the work force for several years) and dealing with equity concerns (the Saskatchewan native law programme is particularly important in this respect). The admission committees will look at additional considerations in these cases.

Professional law schools (there are 20 in Canada) offer three year courses leading to the LL.B. or B.C.L., and in a few cases four year combined LL.B./B.C.L. degrees. The programmes are made up of a combination of compulsory and optional courses. Courses on contract, tort, property (real and personal), commercial law and criminal law are normally included. Courses on legal research and writing and legal institutions are usually included in the first year programme. There are more options in the second and third years and a student wishing to practise, say, in the corporate field may concentrate in that area. The provincial law societies do not generally recognize professional degrees received outside the country.

After receiving a law degree the would-be lawyers still have some way to go. They must article and pass the Bar Admission Course. This part of the programme is controlled by the law society of the particular province in which the candidate wishes to practise. There is some variation from province to province, but generally it involves a combination of an apprenticeship called articles of clerkship, the completion of further technical courses and comprehensive practice-oriented examinations. The articles are usually served at law firms but governments and the courts also provide for similar clerkships. Having successfully completed the law degree, articles and the Bar Admission Course, the law student may apply for admission to the bar. If the applicant meets the requirements as to age and residence, he or she will be sworn in at a meeting of the law society (called a Convocation in Ontario) or at a special sitting of the Supreme Court of the province. On being admitted to the bar in the common law provinces, a person becomes both a barrister and a solicitor as described in Chapter Seven.

It should be noted that although admission to law school remains very competitive, there is currently an over-supply of lawyers in some jurisdictions. Many recent graduates who are successfully placed in law firms experience stress and overwork as they attempt to work their way up to the security and remuneration of a partnership. However, not all professional law school graduates practise law in traditional law firm settings.

Some work for the government or work as legal counsel for private companies. Some top graduates enter into further academic and specialized study of law and complete LL.M.s and doctorates in the field. Other graduates work in outside but related fields such as business.

Canadian Constitutional Acts

THE CONSTITUTION ACT, 1867
(U.K.) 30 & 31 Vict., c.3.

An Act for the Union of Canada, Nova Scotia and New Brunswick, and the Government thereof; and for Purposes connected therewith. (29th March, 1867)

Whereas the Provinces of Canada, Nova Scotia and New Brunswick have expressed their Desire to be federally united into One Dominion under the Crown of the United Kingdom of Great Britain and Ireland, with a Constitution similar in Principle to that of the United Kingdom:

And whereas such a Union would conduce to the Welfare of the Provinces and promote the Interests of the British Empire:

And whereas on the Establishment of the Union by Authority of Parliament it is expedient, not only that the Constitution of the Legislative Authority in the Dominion be provided for, but also that the Nature of the Executive Government therein be declared:

And whereas it is expedient that Provision be made for the eventual Admission into the Union of other Parts of British North America:

. . .

VI — Distribution of Legislative Powers

POWERS OF THE PARLIAMENT

91. Legislative authority of Parliament of Canada — It shall be lawful for the Queen, by and with the Advice and Consent of the Senate and House of Commons, to make Laws for the Peace, Order, and good Government of Canada, in relation to all Matters not coming within the Classes of Subjects by this Act assigned exclusively to the Legislatures of the Provinces; and for greater Certainty, but not so as to restrict the Generality of the foregoing Terms of this Section, it is hereby declared that (notwithstanding anything in this Act) the exclusive Legislative Authority of the Parliament of Canada extends to all Matters coming within the Classes of Subjects next hereinafter enumerated; that is to say,

1A   The Public Debt and Property.
2   The Regulation of Trade and Commerce.
2A   Unemployment insurance.
3   The raising of Money by any Mode or System of Taxation.
4   The borrowing of Money on the Public Credit.
5   Postal Service.
6   The Census and Statistics.
7   Militia, Military and Naval Service, and Defence.
8   The fixing of and providing for the Salaries and Allowances of Civil and other Officers of the Government of Canada.
9   Beacons, Buoys, Lighthouses, and Sable Island.
10   Navigation and Shipping.
11   Quarantine and the Establishment and Maintenance of Marine Hospitals.
12   Sea Coast and Inland Fisheries.
13   Ferries between a Province and any British or Foreign Country or between Two Provinces.
14   Currency and Coinage.
15   Banking, Incorporation of Banks, and the Issue of Paper Money.
16   Savings Banks.
17   Weights and Measures.
18   Bills of Exchange and Promissory Notes.
19   Interest.
20   Legal Tender.
21   Bankruptcy and Insolvency.
22   Patents of Invention and Discovery.
23   Copyrights.
24   Indians, and Lands reserved for the Indians.
25   Naturalization and Aliens.
26   Marriage and Divorce.
27   The Criminal Law, except the Constitution of Courts of Criminal Jurisdiction, but including the Procedure in Criminal Matters.
28   The Establishment, Maintenance, and Management of Penitentiaries.
29   Such Classes of Subjects as are expressly excepted in the Enumeration of the Classes of Subjects by this Act assigned exclusively to the Legislatures of the Provinces.

And any Matter coming within any of the Classes of Subjects enumerated in this Section shall not be deemed to come within the Class of Matters of a local or private Nature comprised in the Enumeration of the Classes of Subjects by this Act assigned exclusively to the Legislatures of the Provinces

EXCLUSIVE POWERS OF PROVINCIAL LEGISLATURES

92. Subjects of Exclusive provincial Legislation — In each province the Legislature may exclusively make Laws in relation to Matters coming within the Classes of Subject next hereinafter enumerated; that is to say,

2   Direct Taxation within the Province in order to the raising of a Revenue for Provincial Purposes.

3   The borrowing of Money on the sole Credit of the Province.

4   The Establishment and Tenure of Provincial Offices and the Appointment and Payment of Provincial Officers.

5   The Management and Sale of the Public Lands belonging to the Province and of the Timber and Wood thereon.

6   The Establishment, Maintenance, and Management of Public and Reformatory Prisons in and for the Province.

7   The Establishment, Maintenance, and Management of Hospitals, Asylums, Charities, and Eleemosynary Institutions in and for the Province, other than Marine Hospitals.

8   Municipal Institutions in the Province.

9   Shop, Saloon, Tavern, Auctioneer, and other Licences in order to the raising of a Revenue for Provincial, Local, or Municipal Purposes.

10   Local Works and Undertakings other than such as are of the following Classes:

(a)   Lines of Steam or other Ships, Railways, Canals, Telegraphs, and other Works and Undertakings connecting the Province with any other or others of the Provinces, or extending beyond the Limits of the Province:

(b)   Lines of Steam Ships between the Province and any British or Foreign Country:

(c)   Such Works as, although wholly situate within the Province, are before or after their Execution declared by the Parliament of Canada to be for the general Advantage of Canada or for the Advantage of Two or more of the Provinces.

11   The Incorporation of Companies with Provincial Objects.

12   The Solemnization of Marriage in the Province.
13   Property and Civil Rights in the Province.
14   The Administration of Justice in the Province, including the Constitution, Maintenance, and Organization of Provincial Courts, both of Civil and of Criminal Jurisdiction, and including Procedure in Civil Matters in those Courts.
15   The Imposition of Punishment by Fine, Penalty, or Imprisonment for enforcing any Law of the Province made in relation to any Matter coming within any of the Classes of Subjects enumerated in this Section.
16   Generally all Matters of a merely local or private Nature in the Province.

THE CANADA ACT 1982, INCLUDING THE CONSTITUTION ACT (U.K.), 1982 c.11

An Act to give effect to a request by the Senate and House of Commons of Canada. Whereas Canada has requested and consented to the enactment of an Act of the Parliament of the United Kingdom to give effect to the provisions hereinafter set forth and the Senate and the House of Commons of Canada in Parliament assembled have submitted an address to Her Majesty requesting that Her Majesty may graciously be pleased to cause a Bill to be laid before the Parliament of the United Kingdom for that Purpose.

Be it therefore enacted by the Queen's Most Excellent Majesty, by and with the advice and consent of the Lords Spiritual and Temporal, and Commons, in this present Parliament assembled, and by the authority of the same, as follows:

1. The *Constitution Act, 1982* set out in schedule B to this Act is hereby enacted for and shall have the force of law in Canada and shall come unto force as provided in that Act.

2. No Act of the Parliament of the United Kingdom passed after the *Constitution Act, 1982* comes into force shall extend to Canada as part of its law.

3. So far as it is not contained in Schedule B, the French version of this Act is set out in Schedule A to this Act and has the same authority in Canada as the English version thereof.

4. This Act may be cited as the *Canada Act 1982*.

SCHEDULE B
CONSTITUTION ACT, 1982

Part I
Canadian Charter of Rights and Freedoms

GUARANTEE OF RIGHTS AND FREEDOMS

1. Rights and Freedoms in Canada — The *Canadian Charter of Rights and Freedoms* guarantees the rights and freedoms set out in it subject only to such reasonable limits prescribed by law as can be demonstrably justified in a free and democratic society.

FUNDAMENTAL FREEDOMS

2. Fundamental freedoms — Everyone has the following fundamental freedoms:

  (a)   freedom of conscience and religion;
  (b)   freedom of thought, belief, opinion and expression, including freedom of the press and other means of communication;
  (c)   freedom of peaceful assembly; and
  (d)   freedom of association.

DEMOCRATIC RIGHTS

3. Democratic rights of citizens — Every citizen of Canada has the right to vote in an election of members of the House of Commons or of a legislative assembly and to be qualified for membership therein.

4.(1) Maximum duration of legislative bodies — No House of Commons and no legislative assembly shall continue for longer than five years from the date fixed for the return of the writs at a general election of its members.

(2) Continuation in special circumstances — In time of real or apprehended war, invasion or insurrection, a House of Commons may be continued by Parliament and a legislative assembly may be continued by the legislature beyond five years if such continuation is not opposed by the votes of more than one-third of the members of the House of Commons or the legislative assembly, as the case may be.

5. Annual sitting of legislative bodies — There shall be a sitting of Parliament and of each legislature at least once every twelve months.

MOBILITY RIGHTS

6.(1) **Mobility of citizens** — Every citizen of Canada has the right to enter, remain in, and leave Canada.

(2) **Rights to move and gain livelihood** — Every citizen of Canada and every person who has the status of a permanent resident of Canada has the right

(a)   to move to and take up residence in an province; and
(b)   to pursue the gaining of livelihood in any province.

(3) **Limitation** — The rights specified in subsection (2) are subject to

(a)   any laws or practices of general application in force in a province other than those that discriminate among persons primarily on the basis of province of present or previous residence; and
(b)   any laws providing for reasonable residency requirements as a qualification for the receipt of publicly provided social services.

(4) **Affirmative action programs** — Subsections (2) and (3) do not preclude any law, program or activity that has as its object the amelioration in a province of conditions of individuals in that province who are socially or economically disadvantaged if the rate of employment in that province is below the rate of employment in Canada.

LEGAL RIGHTS

7. Life, liberty and security of person — Everyone has the right to life, liberty, and security of the person and the right not to be deprived thereof except in accordance with the principles of fundamental justice.

8. Search or seizure — Everyone has the right to be secure against unreasonable search or seizure.

9. Detention or imprisonment — Everyone has the right not to be arbitrarily detained or imprisoned.

10. Arrest or detention — Everyone has the right on arrest or detention

(a)   to be informed promptly of the reason therefor;
(b)   to retain and instruct counsel without delay and to be informed of that right; and

(c)   to have the validity of the detention determined by way of *habeas corpus* and to be released if the detention is not lawful.

11. Proceedings in criminal and penal matters — Any person charged with an offence has the right

(a)   to be informed without unreasonable delay of the specific offence;

(b)   to be tried within a reasonable time;

(c)   not to be compelled to be a witness in a proceedings against that person in respect of the offence;

(d)   to be presumed innocent until proven guilty according to law in a fair and public hearing by an independent and impartial tribunal;

(e)   not to be denied reasonable bail without just cause;

(f)   except in the case of an offence under military law tried before a military tribunal, to the benefit of trial by jury where the maximum punishment for the offence is imprisonment for five years or a more severe punishment;

(g)   not to be found guilty on account of any act or omission unless, at the time of the act or omission, it constituted an offence under Canadian or International law or was criminal according to the general principles of law recognized by the community of nations;

(h)   if finally acquitted of the offence, not to be tried for it again and, if finally found guilty and punished for the offence, not to be tried or punished for it again; and

(i)   if found guilty of the offence and if punishment for the offence has been varied between the time of commission and the time of sentencing, to the benefit of the lesser punishment.

12. Treatment or punishment — Everyone has the right not to be subjected to any cruel or unusual treatment or punishment.

13. Self-crimination — A witness who testifies in any proceedings has the right not to have any incriminating evidence so given used to incriminate that witness in any other proceedings, except in a prosecution for perjury or for the giving of contradictory evidence.

14. Interpreter — A party or witness in any proceedings who does not understand or speak the language in which the proceedings are conducted or who is deaf has the right to the assistance of an interpreter.

EQUALITY RIGHTS

15.(1) **Equality before and under law and equal protection and bene-fit of law** — Every individual is equal before and under the law and has the right to the equal protection and equal benefit of the law without discrimination and, in particular, without discrimination based on race, national or ethnic origin, colour, religion, sex, age, or mental or physical disability.

(2) **Affirmative action programs** — Subsection (1) does not preclude any law, program or activity that has as its object the amelioration of conditions of disadvantaged individuals or groups including those that are disadvantaged because or race, national or ethnic origin, colour, religion, sex, age, or mental or physical disability.

OFFICIAL LANGUAGES OF CANADA

16.(1) **Official languages of Canada** — English and French are the official languages of Canada and have equality of status and equal rights and privileges as to their use in all institutions of the Parliament and government of Canada.

(2) **Official languages of New Brunswick** — English and French are the official languages of New Brunswick and have equality of status and equal rights and privileges as to the use in all institutions of the legislature and government of New Brunswick.

(3) **Advancement of status and use** — Nothing in this Charter limits the authority of Parliament or of a legislature to advance the equality of status or use of English and French.

16.1(1) **English and French linguistic communities in New Brunswick** — The English linguistic community and the French linguistic community in New Brunswick have equality of status and equal rights and privileges, including the right to distinct educational institutions and such distinct cultural institutions as are necessary for the preservation and promotion of those communities.

(2) **Role of the legislature and government of New Brunswick** — The role of the legislature and the government of New Brunswick to preserve and promote the status, rights and privileges referred to in subsection (1) is affirmed.

17.(1) **Proceedings of Parliament** — Everyone has the right to use English or French in any debates or other proceedings of Parliament.

(2) **Proceedings of New Brunswick legislature** — Everyone has the right to use English or French in any debate and other proceeding of the legislature of New Brunswick.

18.(1) **Parliamentary statutes and records** — The statutes, records and journals of Parliament shall be printed and published in English and French and both language versions are equally authoritative.

(2) **New Brunswick statutes and records** — The statutes, records and journals of New Brunswick shall be printed and published in English and French and both language versions are equally authoritative.

19.(1) **Proceedings in courts established by Parliament** — Either English or French may be used by any person in, or in any pleading in or process issuing from, any court established by Parliament.

(2) **Proceedings in New Brunswick courts** — Either English or French may be used by any person in, or in any pleading in or process issuing from, any court of New Brunswick.

20.(1) **Communications by public with federal institutions** — Any member of the public of Canada has the right to communicate with, and to receive available services from, any head or central office of an institution of the Parliament or government of Canada in English or French, and has the same right with respect to any other office of any such institution where

(a) there is significant demand for communications with and services from that office in such language; or

(b) due to the nature of the office, it is reasonable that communications with and services from that office be available in both English and French.

(2) **Communications by public with New Brunswick institutions** — Any member of the public in New Brunswick has the right to communicate with, and to receive available services from, any office of an institution of the legislature or government of New Brunswick in English or French.

21. Continuation of existing constitutional provisions — Nothing in sections 16 to 20 abrogates or derogates from any right, privilege, or obligation with respect to the English and French languages, or either of them, that exists or is continued by virtue of any other provision of the Constitution of Canada.

22. Rights and privileges preserved — Nothing in sections 16 to 20 abrogates or derogates from any legal or customary right or privilege acquired or enjoyed either before or after the coming into force of this Charter with respect to any language that is not English or French.

MINORITY LANGUAGE EDUCATIONAL RIGHTS

23.(1) **Language of instruction** — Citizens of Canada

   (a)   whose first language learned and still understood is that of the English or French linguistic minority population of the province in which they reside, or
   (b)   who have received their primary school instruction in Canada in English or French and reside in a province where the language in which they received that instruction is the language of the English or French linguistic minority population of the province,

have the right to have their children receive primary and secondary school instruction in that language in that province.

(2) **Continuity of language instruction** — Citizens of Canada of whom any child has received or is receiving primary or secondary school instruction in English or French in Canada, have the right to have all their children receive primary and secondary school instruction in the same language.

(3) **Application where numbers warrant** — The right of citizens of Canada under subsections (1) and (2) to have their children receive primary and secondary school instruction in the language of the English or French linguistic minority population of a province

   (a)   applies wherever in the province the number of children of citizens who have such a right is sufficient to warrant the provision to them out of public funds of minority language instruction; and
   (b)   includes, where the number of children so warrants, the right to have them receive that instruction in minority language educational facilities provided out of public funds.

ENFORCEMENT

24.(1) **Enforcement of guaranteed rights and freedoms** — Anyone whose rights or freedoms, as guaranteed by this Charter, have been infringed or denied may apply to a court of competent jurisdiction to obtain such remedy as the court considers appropriate and just in the circumstances.

(2) **Exclusion of evidence bringing adminstration of justice into disrepute** — Where, in proceedings under subsection (1) a court concludes that evidence was obtained in a manner that infringed or denied any rights or freedoms guaranteed by this Charter, the evidence shall be excluded if it is established that, having regard to all the cicumstances, the admission of it in the proceedings would bring the administration of justice into disrepute.

GENERAL

25. Aboriginal rights and freedoms not affected by Charter — The guarantee in this Charter of certain rights and freedoms shall not be construed so as to abrogate or derogate from any aboriginal, treaty or other rights or freedoms that pertain to the aboriginal peoples of Canada including

(a) any rights or freedoms that have been recognized by the Royal Proclamation of October 7, 1763; and

(b) any rights or freedoms that now exist by way of land claims agreements or may be so acquired.

26. Other rights and freedoms not affected by Charter — The guarantee in this Charter of certain rights and freedoms shall not be construed as denying the existence of any other rights and freedoms that exist in Canada.

27. Multicultural heritage — This Charter shall be interpreted in a manner consistent with the preservation and enhancement of the multicultural heritage of Canadians.

28. Rights guaranteed equally to both sexes — Notwithstanding anything in this Charter, the rights and freedoms referred to in it are guaranteed equally to male and female persons.

29. Rights respecting certain schools preserved — Nothing in this Charter abrogates or derogates from any rights or privileges guaranteed by or under the Constitution of Canada in respect of denominational, separate, or dissentient schools.

30. Application to territories and territorial authorities — A reference in this Charter to a province or to the legislative assembly or legislature of a province shall be deemed to include a reference to the Yukon Territory and the Northwest Territories, or to the appropriate legislative authority thereof, as the case may be.

31. Legislative powers not extended — Nothing in this Charter extends the legislative powers of any body or authority.

APPLICATION OF CHARTER

32.(1) **Application of Charter** — This Charter applies

    (a) to the Parliament and government of Canada in respect of all matters within the authority of Parliament including all matters relating to the Yukon Territory and Northwest Territories; and

    (b) to the legislatures and governments of each province in respect of all matters within the authority of the legislature of each province.

(2) **Exception** — Notwithstanding subsection (1), section 15 shall not have effect until three years after this section comes into force.

33.(1) **Exception where express declaration** — Parliament or the legislature of a province may expressly declare in an Act of Parliament or of the legislature, as the case may be, that the Act or a provision thereof shall operate notwithstanding a provision included in section 2 or sections 7 to 15 of this Charter.

(2) **Operation of exception** — An Act or a provision of an Act in respect of which a declaration made under this section is in effect shall have such operation as it would have but for the provision of this Charter referred to in the declaration.

(3) **Five year limitation** — A declaration made under subsection (1) shall cease to have effect five years after it comes into force or on such earlier date as may be specified in the declaration.

(4) **Re-enactment** — Parliament or the legislature of a province may re-enact a declaration made under subsection (1).

(5) **Five year limitation** — Subsection (3) applies in respect of re-enactment made under subsection (4).

CITATION

34. Citation — This Part may be cited as the *Canadian Charter of Rights and Freedoms*.

Part II
Rights of the Aboriginal Peoples of Canada

35.(1) **Recognition of existing aboriginal and treaty rights** — The existing aboriginal and treaty rights of the aboriginal peoples of Canada are hereby recognized and affirmed.

(2) **Definition of "aboriginal peoples of Canada"** — In this Act, "aboriginal peoples of Canada" includes the Indian, Inuit and Metis peoples of Canada.

(3) **Land claims agreements** — For greater certainty, in subsection (1) "treaty rights" includes rights that now exist by way of land claims agreements or may be so acquired.

(4) **Aboriginal and treaty rights are guaranteed equally to both sexes** — Notwithstanding any other provision of this Act, the aboriginal and treaty rights referred to in subsection (1) are guaranteed equally to male and female persons.

35.1 Commitment to participation in constitutional conference — The government of Canada and the provincial governments are committed to the principle that, before any amendment is made to Class 24 of section 91 of the *Constitution Act, 1867*, to section 25 of this Act or to this Part

(a) a constitutional conference that includes in its agenda an item relating to the proposed amendment, composed of the Prime Minister of Canada and the first ministers of the provinces, will be convened by the Prime Minister of Canada; and

(b) the Prime Minister of Canada will invite representatives of the aboriginal peoples of Canada to participate in the discussions on that item.

. . .

Part V
Procedure for Amending Constitution of Canada

38.(1) **General procedure for amending Constitution of Canada** — An amendment to the Constitution of Canada may be made by proclamation issued by the Governor General under the Great Seal of Canada where so authorized by

(a)   resolutions of the Senate and the House of Commons; and

(b)   resolutions of the legislative assemblies of at least two-thirds of the provinces that have, in the aggregate, according to the then latest general census, at least fifty per cent of the population of the provinces.

(2) **Majority of members** — An amendment made under subsection (1) that derogates from the legislative powers, the proprietary rights or any other rights or privileges of the legislature or government of a province shall require a resolution supported by a majority of the members of each of the Senate, the House of Commons and the legislative assemblies required under subsection (1).

(3) **Expression of dissent** — An amendment referred to in subsection (2) shall not have effect in a province the legislative assembly of which has expressed its dissent thereto by resolution supported by a majority of its members prior to the issue of the proclamation to which the amendment relates unless that legislative assembly, subsequently, by resolution supported by a majority of its members, revokes its dissent and authorizes the amendment.

(4) **Revocation of dissent** — A resolution of dissent made for the purposes of subsection (3) may be revoked at any time before or after the issue of the proclamation to which it relates.

39.(1) **Restriction on proclamation** — A proclamation shall not be issued under section 38(1) before the expiration of one year from the adoption of the resolution initiating the amendment procedure thereunder, unless the legislative assembly of each province has previously adopted a resolution of assent or dissent.

(2) **Idem** — A proclamation shall not be issued under section 38(1) after the expiration of three years from the adoption of the resolution initiating the amendment procedure thereunder.

40. Compensation — Where an amendment is made under subsection 38(1) that transfers provincial legislative powers relating to education or other cultural matters from provincial legislatures to Parliament, Canada shall provide reasonable compensation to any province to which the amendment does not apply.

41. Amendment by unanimous consent — An amendment to the Constitution of Canada in relation to the following matters may be made by proclamation issued by the Governor General under the Great Seal of Canada only where authorized by resolutions of the Senate and House of Commons and of the legislative assemblies of each province:

(a) the office of the Queen, the Governor General, and the Lieutenant Governor of a province;

(b) the right of a province to a number of members in the House of Commons not less than the number of Senators by which the province is entitled to be represented at the time this Part comes into force;

(c) subject to section 43, the use of the English or the French language;

(d) the composition of the Supreme Court of Canada; and

(e) an amendment to this Part.

42.(1) **Amendment by general procedure** — An amendment to the Constitution of Canada in relation to the following matters may be made only in accordance with subsection 38(1):

(a) the principle of proportionate representation of the provinces in the House of Commons prescribed by the Constitution of Canada;

(b) the powers of the Senate and the method of selecting Senators;

(c) the number of members by which a province is entitled to be represented in the Senate and the residence qualifications of Senators;

(d) subject to paragraph 41(d), the Supreme Court of Canada;

(e) the extension of existing provinces into the territories; and

(f) notwithstanding any other law or practice, the establishment of new provinces.

(2) **Exceptions** — Subsections 38(2) to 38(4) do not apply in respect of amendments in relation to matters referred to in subsection (1).

43. Amendment provisions relating to some but not all provinces — An amendment to the Constitution of Canada in relation to any provision that applies to one or more, but not all provinces, including

(a) any alteration to boundaries between provinces, and
(b) any amendment to any provisions that relate to the use of the English or the French language within a province

may be made by proclamation issued by the Governor General under the Great Seal of Canada only where so authorized by resolutions of the Senate and House of Commons and of the legislative assembly of each province to which the amendment applies.

44. Amendments by Parliament — Subject to sections 41 and 42, Parliament may exclusively make laws amending the Constitution of Canada in relation to the executive government of Canada or the Senate and House of Commons.

45. Amendments by provincial legislatures — Subject to section 41, the legislature of each province may exclusively make laws amending the constitution of the province.

46.(1) Initiation of amendment procedures — The procedures for amendment under sections 38, 41, 42, and 43 may be initiated either by the Senate or the House of Commons or by the legislative assembly of province.

(2) **Revocation of authorization —** A resolution of assent for the purposes of this Part may be revoked at any time before the issue of a proclamation authorized by it.

47.(1) Amendments without Senate resolution — An amendment to the Constitution of Canada made by proclamation under sections 38, 41, 42, or 43 may be made without a resolution of the Senate authorizing the issue of the proclamation if, within one hundred and eighty days after the adoption by the House of Commons of a resolution authorizing its issue, the Senate has not adopted such a resolution and if, at any time after the expiration of that period, the House of Commons again adopts the resolution.

(2) **Computation of period —** Any period when Parliament is prorogued or dissolved shall not be counted in computing the one hundred and eighty day period referred to in subsection (1).

48. Advice to issue proclamation — The Queen's Privy Council for Canada shall advise the Governor General to issue a proclamation under this part forthwith on the adoption of the resolutions required for an amendment made by proclamation under this Part.

49. Constitutional conference — A constitutional conference of the Prime Minister of Canada and the first ministers shall be convened by the Prime Minister of Canada within fifteen years after this Part comes into force to review the provisions of this Part.

. . .

Part VII
General

52.(1) **Primacy of the Constitution of Canada** — The Constitution of Canada is the supreme law of Canada, and any law that is inconsistent with the provisions of the Constitution is, to the extent of the inconsistency, of no force or effect.

(2) **Constitution of Canada** — The Constitution of Canada includes

(a)   the *Canada Act 1982*, including this Act;
(b)   the Acts and orders referred to in the Schedule; and
(c)   any amendment to any Act or order referred to in paragraph (a) or (b).

(3) **Amendments to Constitution of Canada** — Amendments to the Constitution of Canada shall be made only in accordance with the authority contained in the Constitution of Canada.

60. Short title and citations — This Act may be cited as the *Constitution Act, 1982*, and the *Constitution Acts 1867 to 1975* (No. 2) and this Act may be cited together as the *Constitution Acts, 1867 to 1982*.

Index